GHOSTS IN THE MIRROR

WORKS BY ALAIN ROBBE-GRILLET
Published by Grove Weidenfeld

The Erasers
Ghosts in the Mirror
Jealousy and *In the Labyrinth*
Last Year at Marienbad
La Maison de Rendez-vous and *Djinn*
Project for a Revolution in New York
Recollections of the Golden Triangle
Snapshots
Topology of a Phantom City
The Voyeur

GHOSTS
IN THE
MIRROR

Alain Robbe-Grillet

Translated from the French
by Jo Levy

Grove Weidenfeld
New York

Published by Grove Weidenfeld
A division of Grove Press, Inc.
841 Broadway
New York, N.Y. 10003-4793

Originally published in France under the title *Le Miroir qui revient* by
Les Editions de Minuit, Paris, 1984.

Library of Congress Cataloging-in-Publication Data

Robbe-Grillet, Alain, 1922–
    [Miroir qui revient. English]
    Ghosts in the mirror / Alain Robbe-Grillet ; translated from the
French by Jo Levy.
       p.   cm.
    Translation of: Le miroir qui revient.
    ISBN 0-8021-1036-3
    1. Robbe-Grillet, Alain, 1922–   —Biography. 2. Novelists,
French—20th century—Biography. I. Title.
PQ2635.O117Z47513   1991
843'.914—dc20
[B]   90-19100
                                          CIP

Manufactured in the United States of America

Printed on acid-free paper

Designed by Paul Chevannes

First American Edition 1991

1   3   5   7   9   10   8   6   4   2

Contents

CONTENTS

CONTENTS

vii

GHOSTS IN THE MIRROR

If I remember rightly, I began writing this book a few months after the publication of *Topologie d'une cité fantôme* (*Topology of a Phantom City*), toward the end of 1976 or the beginning of 1977. And now here we are in the autumn of 1983 and the work has hardly progressed; the forty-odd manuscript pages have always been abandoned for tasks that seemed more urgent. Two novels have appeared in the meantime, and a film—*La Belle Captive*—finished in January this year, screened in mid-February. So, nearly seven years have gone by since I began with the words "I have never spoken of anything but myself . . ."—provocative at the time. The lighting has changed, perspectives have shifted, in some cases inverted; but in fact the same questions still come up, perennial, haunting, maybe pointless. . . . Let's try again, seriously, one more time, before it's too late.

Who was Henri de Corinthe? I've already said I don't think I ever met him, except possibly when I was a very small child. But sometimes, when I do have memories of those brief interviews (in the strict sense of the word: as if through a door accidentally left ajar), I feel my fertile memory could be playing tricks and I might have invented them after the event, if not totally, at least from the scrappy accounts whispered in the family or floating around the old house.

M. de Corinthe, Comte Henri—as my father mostly called him, with an intangible blend of irony and respect—often came to see us, I'm almost sure. . . . Often? Today I really can't work out how often. For example, did he come every month? Or more often? Or did he only visit once or twice a year, his appearances—although fleeting—making such a vivid, lasting impression that everyone thought they were more frequent? And when did these visits actually stop?

But above all, what could he have been doing in our house? What secrets, plans, needs, what kind of expectations or fears, would have associated him with my parents when everything—birth as well as fortune— seemed to separate them? Living such an adventurous life, how and why did he find time to stay for a few hours (a few days?) in such a modest home? Why did my father seem to await his unpredictable arrival with a sort of fervent hope? Whereas when I peeped through the gap in the heavy red living-room curtains and saw him with the illustrious visitor, he looked worried, grief-stricken. And also, although they never admitted it, why did they so obviously try and stop me from meeting him?

It was probably with this albeit uncertain end in view—an attempt at answering such questions as these—that I started writing this autobiography some time ago now. And as I begin reading over the opening pages after a fateful lapse of seven years, I can hardly tell what I wanted to talk about so urgently. This is what happens with writing: at once a lonely, dogged, almost timeless pursuit and an absurd submission to the, as it were, ''worldly'' preoccupations of the moment.

Now, at the beginning of the eighties, there's been a sudden, violent reaction against any attempt to escape the norms of traditional expression-representation; so my imprudent remarks of not so long ago no longer act abrasively to counter a new dogma that was creeping in (antihumanism) but merely seem today to be sliding down the slippery slope of the prevailing discourse, which has been reinstated: the good old eternal discourse of the past that I had fought against so passionately at the outset. In the wave of "regression" breaking over us, my wish, on the contrary, to pass beyond, to "relieve the old guard," is likely to go unnoticed.

So should we now resume the terrorist activities of the years 1955–60? Certainly we should. And yet (I'll explain why later) I persist in copying out these opening lines just as I wrote them in 1977, without changing anything; they are already old-fashioned, in my opinion, since they have so quickly become fashionable.

I have never spoken of anything but myself. From within, and so it has hardly been noticed. Fortunately. Since in the space of two lines I've just used three suspect, shameful, deplorable terms that I myself have largely assisted in discrediting, and this is enough to condemn me once again in the eyes of several of my peers and most of my descendants: "myself," "within," "spoken of."

The second of these apparently innocuous little words alone tiresomely resurrects the humanist myth of depth (the old mole, to us other writers), while the last stealthily brings back the myth of representation, whose contentious case drags on forever. As for the ever detestable "myself," here it is certainly paving the way for an even more frivolous comeback: biography.

So it's no coincidence that at this precise moment I agree to write a *Robbe-Grillet par lui-même,** which a

---

* This volume was originally planned for the *Ecrivains de toujours* series published by Seuil (hence the later mention of "the publisher across the street"). I even had a contract with Paul Flamand, which is still valid. It was

short while ago I would definitely have preferred to leave to others. Everyone nowadays knows that the notion of an author belongs to the reactionary discourse—the discourse of the individual, private property, profit—and that the work of the writer is, on the contrary, anonymous: merely a matter of combinations that could, in a pinch, be left to a machine, since they seem so easily programmable, the human intention being depersonalized in its turn so that it only appears now as a particular phase of the class struggle, which is the mainspring of History in general, as well as the history of the novel.

I myself have done much to promote these reassuring idiocies, and have now decided to refute them because I feel they've had their day: within the space of a few years they have lost any shocking, corrosive, and therefore revolutionary force and have been assimilated as received ideas, fueling the spineless militance of the fashionable journals, yet with their place already prepared in the glorious family vaults of the literature textbooks. Ideology, always masked, changes its face with ease. It is a hydra-mirror whose severed head quickly reappears, presenting the adversary who thought himself victorious the image of his own face.

Copying this strategy, I'm going to make use of the monster's remains too: see through his eyes, hear through his ears, and speak through his mouth (steep my arrows in his blood). I don't believe in Truth. It only serves bureaucracy, that is, oppression. The moment a bold theory stated in the heat of battle has become dogma, it instantly loses its attraction and violence, and by the same token, its efficacy. It ceases to ferment liberty, discovery; nicely and thoughtlessly, it contributes one more stone to the edifice of the established order.

---

only the unexpected turn the text took as it was being composed that made it unsuitable for this series of little books with their prescribed dimensions and numerous illustrations, for which I am therefore doing something quite different, concurrently.

And so it's time to pursue other tracks and turn the fine new theory inside out in order to rout the incipient bureaucracy it's secretly harboring. Now that the New Novel defines its values positively, decrees its laws, brings its recalcitrant pupils back to the fold, enlists its guerrillas, excommunicates its freethinkers, there's a pressing need to call everything into question and put the pieces back as they were, to take writing back to its starting point and the author back to his first book: we must once more question the ambiguous role played in the modern narrative by the representation of the world and the expression of a *person* who is simultaneously a physical body, a conscious projection, and an unconscious.

I've been asked so often in interviews and symposia why I write that I ended up seeing the question as belonging to the realm of meaning, of *ratio*, which attempts to impose its intellectual laws (and so its dictatorship) on an activity that is dynamic and therefore always elusive. And in order to fill the silence from which writing comes I simply threw out various idle banalities, devious suggestions that led nowhere, or substituted scintillating metaphors for aphorisms. That was better than scraps of a catechism anyway.

But now that I've decided to take a sidelong look at myself in the space of a small book, the new perspective has suddenly freed me from my old defenses and reticence. I feel so bound up with the life and adventures of Editions de Minuit that in speaking of myself from the publisher across the street, I experience a completely new kind of freedom; I'm lighthearted, cheerful, an irresponsible narrator.

Consequently no definitive, no merely truthful explanation of my written work and films should be expected from these pages (a definitive explanation straight from the author's mouth!)—how they really work, their real significance. I've said I'm not a truthful man, but nor do I tell lies, which would come to the same thing. I'm a sort of resolute, ill-equipped, imprudent explorer who doesn't believe in the previous existence or stability of the country in which he is mapping out a possible road, day by day. I'm not an intellectual guru but a companion on the path of discovery and hazardous research. And it is still a work of fiction that I venture here.

When I was a child, for a long time I thought I didn't like the sea. Every night I drifted off to look for a tranquil unfenced garden to fall asleep in, and the image of the paternal Haut-Jura formed most often in my mind: a hollow filled with moss-grown rocks or lined with cushions of saxifrage, gentle slopes, foothills covered with short grass, smooth as a park sown with gentians and soldanellas, where large fawn-colored cows moved about slowly to a peaceful tinkling of bells among patches of immutable forest, like a stage set. Order. Rest. Everlasting quiet. I could abandon myself to sleep.

The ocean was turmoil and uncertainty, a realm of insidious perils where flaccid, viscous creatures mated in the muffled waves. And this was precisely the ocean that filled the nightmares I fell into the moment I lost consciousness, soon to wake up with screams of terror that didn't always dispel these confused phantoms I couldn't even describe. My mother gave me linctus of bromide. Her anxious eyes in some way confirmed the dangers I had only escaped for the time being, which were lying in wait for me again in the dark, lurking behind my own eyes. Hallucinations, nocturnal delirium, intermittent sleepwalking—I was a calm child who slept restlessly.

We lived for a part of the year in my maternal family's house, where I was born, a big house surrounded by a walled garden that seemed huge at the time; it was on the outskirts of Brest in what was then the country. From the windows of the room where I slept, you could see the whole Rade de Brest above the trees. On our walks, which sometimes lasted several days, we went from Brignogan, the river mouth, Saint-Mathieu, and the Ile d'Ouessant right up to the Pointe du Raz, in the wind, on the cold beaches, across heaps of jumbled rocks, or along the crumbling, slippery coastguard paths on the edge of the precipice.

We spent August in a little village on the Quiberon Peninsula, and there too we preferred the Côte Sauvage, which really was still wild before the war and made us only too ready to believe the legends: whirlpools with subterranean crevices leading to the open sea, where you could drown with your legs tugged under by the long strands of seaweed coiling around them; flood tides trapping you at the foot of a smooth vertical wall; waves from the deep, invisible on the surface, reaching right up to the top of the highest cliff, sucking you down and swallowing you up. Needless to say, I didn't learn canoeing or sailing, I never even learned to swim. In the mountains, from the time I was twelve, with no ski slopes or lifts, I was perfectly at ease and quite reckless on my skis.

Any amateur psychologist will be delighted to recognize in the facile contrast between the Jura and the Atlantic—gentle vale of mossy hollows versus bottomless pit where the octopus lies in wait—the two traditional opposed images of the female sex. I wouldn't like him to think that he's discovered this unbeknownst to me. And while we're at it, let's draw his attention to the phonetic similarity of *vague* (wave) and *vagin* (vagina), and also to the etymology of the word *cauchemar* (nightmare), whose root *mare* means "sea" in Latin, but in Dutch, "nocturnal phantoms."

The room where I slept in the small Parisian apartment on Rue Gassendi was separated by a glass double door from the dining room, where my mother would stay up late into the night reading her massive daily dose of papers ranging from *La Liberté* to *L'Action française* (my parents were extreme right-wing anarchists). The translucent red curtain that left me in relative darkness was held open by the back of a chair so that she could keep close watch over my broken sleep. Her gaze, reaching me from time to time above the outspread newspaper, would disturb my solitary pleasures, which already had a strong sadistic tendency. As for the ghosts, they usually appeared opposite me, in a corner of the ceiling, on the same side as the reddened panes; they advanced in steady waves over the pale part of the wall, between a cornice of acanthus leaves and the molding that bordered the dark green wallpaper. The recurrent hallucination moved from left to right in a series of spirals or little waves, or more accurately, like the ornamental frieze sculptors call Vitruvian scrolls. What terrified me was when their seemingly orderly ranks began to tremble, disintegrate, and twist in all directions. But the first steady sinusoid was already enough to frighten me, I so dreaded what was coming next.

It strikes me that I've been saying all this for a long time now, both in my books and in my films, and in a more accurate and convincing way. Obviously this hasn't been noticed, or hardly at all. Obviously it's never bothered me: that wasn't the point of writing.

And yet today I feel a certain pleasure in using the traditional autobiographical form: the ease mentioned by Stendhal in his *Souvenirs d'égotisme* (*Memoirs of an Egotist*), compared with the resistance of the material that characterizes all creativity. And I'm interested in this questionable pleasure on the one hand in that it confirms that I began writing novels to exorcise the ghosts I couldn't come to terms with, and on the other hand, because it makes me see that the bias of fiction is, after all, much more *personal* than the so-called sincerity of confession.

When I reread sentences like "My mother kept close watch over my broken sleep" or "Her gaze would disturb my solitary pleasures," I have an irresistible urge to laugh, as if I were falsifying my past life in order to make it into a nice conventional object according to the canons of the late lamented *Figaro littéraire*: logical, affecting, malleable. Not that these details are inaccurate (far from it, perhaps). But what's wrong is that there aren't enough of them, and they read like a work of fiction; in a word, I don't like what I would call their arrogance. I didn't live them in the imperfect tense, nor with particular adjectives in mind, and what's more, when they actually happened, they were swarming in the midst of an infinite number of other details, the interwoven threads forming a living web. Whereas now I pick out a paltry dozen, each set up on its pedestal, cast in the bronze of a quasi-historical narrative (the past historic is not far away), and arranged in a causal sequence precisely conforming to the ideological tyranny against which my whole work rebels.

We're beginning to see more clearly. First rough point: I write to destroy, by describing them exactly, the nocturnal monsters that threaten to invade my waking life. But—second point—all reality is indescribable, and I know it instinctively: consciousness is structured like our language (and with good reason!); not so the world or the unconscious. I can't use words and phrases to describe what's in front of me, nor what's lurking in my head or in my sex. (Let's leave cinematic images aside for the moment; I'll demonstrate later—if I think of it— that they pose almost the same problems, contrary to what people think.)

Literature is, then—third position—the pursuit of an impossible representation. Knowing this, what can I do? All I can do is organize stories, which are neither

11

metaphors of reality nor analogues but act as *working constructs*. Then the ideology that governs our common consciousness and language structures will no longer be a constraint, a source of failure, since I've reduced it to the status of material.

From this perspective I can see my plan to tell my life story in two different and contradictory ways. Either I insist on grasping the truth, pretending to believe that language can do this (which is the same as admitting language is free), and in that case, all I will ever produce is a *ready-made life story*. Alternatively, I will replace the biographical details with working constructs explicitly expressing an ideology, but over these and thanks to these I will this time be able to exercise my influence. The second method produces *La Jalousie* (*Jealousy*) or *Projet pour une révolution* (*Project for a Revolution in New York*). The first, alas, the present work.

No, that's not quite true either, since it will by now be obvious that this work isn't going to be restricted to a few trite memories offered as gospel truth. On the contrary, it must accompany me from critical essay to novel, from book to film, in a continual questioning, in which the sea and fear will become in turn mere working constructs in the text; and not solely in such and such a work mentioned, where these textual objects determine theme or structure, but also in this treatise itself, which is why I previously called it fiction.

So, I was talking about fear. Very early on it came to play a large part in my infrequent reading as an adolescent. My sister (who read a lot) and I (who always read the same books over and over again) had been brought up on English literature from an early age. I've often mentioned Lewis Carroll as one of the main companions of my youth. More rarely I've spoken of Rudyard Kipling, though *Kim* and *The Jungle Books* were not as precious to me as his Indian tales, particularly the ones where soldiers were terrorized by morbid apparitions. Without having laid eyes on them for thirty or forty years, I could retell the story of the legion lost in the night meeting another British patrol that had been wiped out in an ambush long ago. I can still hear the hoofbeats—a hundred dead horsemen stamping along the mountainside as they stumble over the stones that mark their own graves. Also the story of Colonel Gadsby, parading at the head of his regiment, who constantly sees himself falling from the saddle, crushed under the hooves of the thousand horses of his dragoons riding at full gallop behind him. And that other officer, pursued by a phantom rickshaw in which an abandoned mistress is weeping, driven to suicide by despair. Or the man who at 104 degrees in the shade puts a sharp spur in his bed in an attempt to escape the frightful visions—never described—to which he falls prey the moment he goes to sleep, and which finally kill him.

I grew up on intimate terms with these specters. They were quite simply part of my normal world, mixed up with spirits from Breton legends or from the ghost stories my maternal grandmother's sister, our "godmother," used to tell us in the evening to send us to sleep: sailors lost at sea coming back to drag the living from their beds by the feet; the *ankou*'s cart, whose creaking and jolting announces the imminent death of the nocturnal stroller lost in a web of sunken lanes that he thought he knew; enchanted spaces, bewitched objects, omens and signs, not to mention the countless tormented souls keening on the heaths or in the marshes, rattling the shutters of your room till daybreak when there isn't a breath of air, and stirring up the water in the basins where the washing's been left to soak.

As the years and the stories went by, this family continued to grow, ever ready to welcome new presences quite naturally, from Corinthe's pale fiancée to the cursed Dutchman rushing through the night on the deck of his unmanned ship, his red sails outspread over the phosphorescent waves. And here comes the ocean, back again so soon. O Death, old captain, it is time to weigh anchor . . .

And here's the young Comte de Corinthe battling the rising tide, riding his white horse, its sparkling mane wreathed with spray storm-torn from the crest of the waves. And here's Tristan, wounded, delirious, waiting in vain for the ship that will bring Iseult the Fair back to Lyoness. And now here's Caroline de Saxe, her lifeless body drifting among the golden, rippling seaweed.

Characters in novels or films are also kinds of phantoms: you see them or hear them, you can never grasp them, if you try you pass right through them. Their existence is suspect, insistent, like that of the unquiet dead forced by some evil spell or divine vengeance to live the same scenes from their tragic destiny over and over again. So Mathias in *Le Voyeur* (*The Voyeur*), for instance, whom I've often come across wheeling his squeaky bike on the cliff paths among tufts of close-cropped gorse, would simply be a wandering soul, just like the absent husband in *La Jalousie* and the heros who people *Marienbad*, *L'Immortelle* (*The Immortal One*), or *L'Homme qui ment* and so obviously come from the land of shades. At any rate, this is one of the most plausible "explications" of why they don't look "natural," why they seem remote, disoriented, out of place, of their relentless pursuit of goodness knows what, which they seem unable either to abandon or to carry through, as if they were desperately trying to gain access to a fleshly existence that is denied them, trying to enter a veracious world that is closed to them, or else attempting to drag the *other*, all the others, including the innocent reader, into their impossible quest. Stephen Dedalus, the land surveyor K., Stavrogin, or the brothers Karamazov lived like this. These labyrinthine paths, this marking time, these scenes that are repeated over and over again (even death can never again be final), changeless bodies, timelessness, multiple spatial dislocations, finally the theme of the "double," which informs a whole section of our literature and structures *L'Homme qui ment* as well as *L'Eden et après* or *Triangle d'or* (*Recollections of the Golden Triangle*)—aren't these precisely the distinctive signs and natural laws of the eternal regions of the possessed?

I didn't know Henri de Corinthe personally. I probably never even saw him, as I imagine now, in those early years of my childhood at the Maison Noire, where, as my father told me, he came from time to time on a neighborly visit before retiring for the night.

At the time I thought the old house where I was born got its name from the dark granite facade, which was so smooth and hard that no moss or lichen had taken hold on its high vertical wall, except in the joins between the carefully fitted rectangular blocks. When the winter drizzle dampened the surface, they gleamed like coal between the gray branches of the beech trees, where here and there tenacious russet leaves still clung in the endless fine rain.

Corinthe would come up the long, straight drive between the two rows of vertical boles, like the pillars of Constantinople's underground reservoirs in the engraving that graced my room at the head of the bed. His horse's hooves made no sound on the sodden ground as he approached in a sort of silent dance, as if space, saturated with water, had relieved him of his own weight.

My father said that whether on foot or riding his white mount, the man always appeared like this: no sound of heel, sole, or horseshoe signaled his approach;

it was as if his heavy boots and the horse's hooves were wrapped in a thick layer of felt—unless they both had the power to move about without touching the ground, a few millimeters above the road or the black stone staircase or the flagstone floor of the vast dark room at whose far end he is now standing in front of the monumental fireplace where big oak logs burn, his tall silhouette elongated by the fire lighting him from behind, while his huge shadow, flickering with the flames, lengthens, turns paler and paler, reaches to the foot of the stairs that my father, called by a servant, is now descending to go to his late visitor, who is holding out his frozen limbs to the ever changing colors in the hearth.

Guttering paraffin lamp, will-o'-the-wisp on the marshes, pale rider gliding through the mist, murmuring water, a great bird's quick cry of alarm piercing the night nearby, the sudden crackling of the fire breaking out among the dying embers . . . Angélica . . . Angélica . . . Why did you leave me, little flame? Who will console me for your light laugh?

I'm alone in my room. I listen to the nocturnal sounds surrounding the too spacious empty house on all sides. My dark window sways in the wind, framing the bare crowns of the beeches. But over the rustle of the branches against the uncurtained windowpanes, louder than the rain trickling in the valleys and gutters, rising above the heartrending calls of owl or weasel, I can hear muffled thuds from the bowels of the building, like the thrusting of waves against the raised hull of a ship as it drops back into the trough, thuds that seem to come out of the floor, the granite walls, the ancient earth itself, repeated blows, persistent, regular, which must be the slow beating of my own heart.

Down below in the vast flagstoned room whose dim boundaries are defined by the darkness alone, my father paces up and down while the memory of Henri de Corinthe gradually fades. Neither of them says a word, each is lost in his own thoughts, each is alone. . . . The blurred image stays for a few moments more, harder and harder to make out. . . . Then, nothing.

The above passage must be a complete fiction. The family house was simple, relatively large, sheltered by a few trees, but built of wattle and daub since the navy didn't allow anything more substantial in this zone, which was then under the jurisdiction of the naval base. Nevertheless, the repeated thuds shaking the ground are definitely part of my childhood impressions. They could be heard particularly at night, every night for months on end. The hypothesis most often proposed by our grandparents, who were also worried by this phenomenon which was never officially explained, was that it was the result of the excavation work the engineering corps was carrying out under the cliffs, like some giant mole, for the purpose of installing vast underground reservoirs to store the fuel needed by our battle fleet. There was a large fleet based in Brest at the time. The whole town and its surroundings seemed to be under the supreme, mysterious rule of the admiralty.

My grandfather, an affectionate, kind, peaceable man with light blue eyes and a soft blond goatee, who sang "Cherry Blossom Time" in an emotional voice broken by emphysema, had spent all his active life on warships. His cutlass is still up in the attic, as are his heavy camphorwood trunk with its thick brass-bound corners and the identification tag with his name engraved in black on yellow metal: Paul Canu.

A war orphan, he spent his first years in the salt flats at Cotentin, near La Haye-du-Puits, tending cows while reciting to himself short impromptu poems that he wrote for his own amusement. Signing on early with the sailing fleet, he rounded the Horn several times, waited interminably for the trade winds, sailed up the Yellow

River, saw action in the China War and the Annam and Tonkin campaigns. He returned with glorious multicolored medals, the rank of quartermaster second class, some bamboo ashtrays, the remnants of two translucent porcelain tea services smashed during the voyage, and a serious case of tuberculosis that caused his premature death. I only knew him when he was much weakened by illness, but always smiling between coughing fits.

I have an image of him stopping for a moment halfway across the vegetable garden in his slippers, the backs of his hands on his hips; and then sitting at the round table in the kitchen, the leather elbows of his overcoat resting on the flowered oilcloth, meticulously peeling the small windfalls with his penknife to make stewed apples; or in the yard, just as patiently sorting and tying the shallots into bunches, the ones that had been laid out to dry on old jute sacks in the autumn sun; or playing a game of *écarté* with my father in the dining room, with the tame jackdaw perched on his shoulder impishly tipping his peaked cap over his eyes as he played a trump, and then Grandfather would calmly straighten it with a gesture repeated a hundred times, muttering a long string of oaths under his breath. Sometimes, bored with that game, the daw—named Jack, from the imitation of his call that my mother repeated in all directions to get him in at night—would suddenly jump onto the table, snatch a card in his beak, and fly up to the top of the dresser, where he would hide the card in between the pots of red and black currant jam covered with brown paper and tied with thin string. A stepladder had to be fetched so that they could go on with the game.

Grandfather spoke little. I don't remember him ever telling stories about his many trips around the world, of which I know almost nothing apart from some bits and pieces reported by my mother or my aunts: the ship was away for three years, . . . sheep and chickens were reared on board, . . . when they embarked in Toulon the

Breton sailors crossed the whole of France on foot. . . .
One day Admiral Guépratte visited us in person to pin
the Legion of Honor on the chest of the worthy servant
of the Nation and its colonial Empire. I was told it was a
proud day for my grandfather. But I'm not sure now
whether I was present at the scene or whether I was
only told about it. Perhaps it even happened before I
was born.

And so that's all that's left of someone, after such a
short time—and that goes for me too, soon enough, no
doubt: odds and ends, frozen gestures, disconnected
objects, questions in the empty air, a jumble of random snapshots with no real (logical) sequence. That's
death. . . . So to construct a narrative would be a more
or less conscious bid to outwit death. The entire system
of the novel in the last century, with its cumbersome
machinery of continuity, linear chronology, causality,
noncontradiction, was actually a last-ditch attempt to
forget the disintegrated state we were left in when God
withdrew from our souls, an attempt at least to keep up
appearances by replacing the incomprehensible explosion of atoms, of black holes and impasses, with a reassuring, clear, unequivocal constellation woven so
closely that we'd no longer hear death howling between
the stitches, amidst broken threads hastily reknotted.
No objection to this grandiose, unnatural project? . . .
No objection, really?

No objection to the Church? No objection to the Law?
None, except that it's precisely the unacceptable accep-
tance of death itself: death of man, with a small *m*, in the
name of some Ideal—capital *I*—enthroned in the sky,
death of each passing moment (I hardly have time to
say: how beautiful you are), your death, reader, that is,
mine too. Artfully set up as realistic, this reassuring
narrative—spurious (since it speaks in the name of an

eternal truth), totalitarian (since it doesn't leave room for any empty space whatsoever, nor for any plenitude outside the plot)—this bloodsucking narrative, while claiming to save me from my approaching death, is from the start going to convince me that I've already stopped living, once and for all.

Isn't the famous past definite tense, the past "historic," which is of no use in life and yet is the rule in that kind of novel, merely the sudden, definitive glaciation of the most incomplete gestures, the most ephemeral thoughts, the most ambiguous dreams, sense left hanging in the air, tenuous desires, stray or inadmissible memories? The "simple" past is just as simple—as certain and solid—as the tomb. A last flicker of life breathed into this hollow sham could now find expression only in the senseless art of representing oneself and the world as if cast in the same dense, imperishable concrete for all eternity.

Certainly, during the years I was learning to create a form of writing in search of itself (it still is), what was important to me was Sartre's surprising transition from *La Nausée* (*Nausea*) to *L'Age de raison* (*The Age of Reason*). From the opening pages of the so-called *Chemins de la liberté* (*Roads to Freedom*), the newborn, elusive freedom that made Roquentin's body tremble and his mind reel is suddenly brought to a standstill by a past historic that comes crashing down on the characters (and the author?) like a ton of bricks: "Mathieu thought . . ." Mathieu can think what he likes—that he's old, free, a bastard—but as soon as he does it in this grammatical tense, all I've got is an oppressive reading: Mathieu thought he was dead. His very freedom, his most precious possession, thus becomes just one more fatality, an accursed essence that instantly freezes in his veins, since it's as if it had been decided by a god outside the text: traditional narrative technique. We can well imagine François Mauriac's sigh of relief: "So much for M. Jean-Paul Sartre and his freedom!"

What's the modern novel—called the New Novel (we shall soon see why)—doing now? Once more it's a narrative in search of its own coherence. Once more it's the impossible ordering of disparate fragments whose blurred outlines don't fit together. And once more there's the desperate temptation to create a fabric as solid as bronze. . . . Yes, but what's happening in this fabric, the text, is that it has itself become battlefield and stake. Instead of advancing like some blind justice obeying a divine law, deliberately ignoring all the problems that the traditional novel disguises and denies (the present moment, for instance), the text is determined on the contrary to expose publicly and stage accurately the multiple impossibilities with which it is contending and of which it is constructed. So that this internal conflict will soon become (from the 1960s onward) the very subject of the book. Hence the complicated sequences, digressions, cuts and repetitions, aporias, blind alleys, shifts in perspective, various permutations, dislocations, or inversions, etc.

Faced with the absurd or academic—and in any case useless—attempt to say who my grandfather was, I feel like Roquentin faced with the Marquis de Rollebon's lifeless, scattered remains. And like Roquentin on the last page of *La Nausée*, I realize that there's only one decision to make: to write a novel, which of course will not be *L'Age de raison* but *Un Régicide*, for example, or rather *Souvenirs du triangle d'or* . . .

But we haven't got to that point yet, since through sheer perversity I'm still fumbling on with a realistic, biographical, representational venture. For most of the day Grandfather would do crossword puzzles at the kitchen table or on the narrow leaf of his writing desk. He also spent a long time sorting out little bits of paper from his nine drawers made of pale yellow wood with a black border.... Having written this last sentence, I wanted to check that detail (was the border black, or only the knobs?), so I went down to the ground floor of the Spartan home in Normandy where I've been working for fifteen years. There are only five little drawers behind the drop leaf, which also looks like a drawer from the outside. What does it matter? Anyway, this piece of furniture is no longer in Brest, where everything has changed, even the design of the old house, which was rebuilt after the war and is now nothing like the house of the thirties . . .

And now there's more confusion as I copy out this passage a month later in my apartment on Bleecker Street in New York and I remember two quite different desks: one from Kerangoff and one from Le Mesnil-au-Grain. Besides, a cabinetmaker has recently restored one of them.

Confronted with a world that was changing too fast for him, Grandfather would say, "It's good to grow old." And yet as he was dying he murmured, sighing, "I still had so many things left to do!" Today the echo of that "still" brings a lump to my throat. He must have been worrying about the scraps of paper in his drawers, the small windfalls, the delicate pink-orange skin peeling off the shallots. We never finish putting things in order.

I'm not sure; the phrase "It's good to grow old" must have been my other, much older grandfather's: Ulysse Robbe-Grillet, my father's father, a retired teacher (in Arbois), whom we called Grandfather Robbe to distinguish him from the first. I don't remember anything about him except his bulky frame and his big moustache in faded photos.

I really didn't know Grandfather Canu any better. But I do remember liking him. He, I am told, wasn't very interested in me. I had long curly hair, like a girl, and was good at wheedling. I would cry if I skinned my knees. I was afraid to cross the dark courtyard at night to get to the old-fashioned outhouse, even though it was only ten meters away. I would never be a soldier, nor wield the heavy cutlass. . . . (Beware: double trap for the psychomachine!) Come to think of it, I don't think my gentle grandfather, the quartermaster, ever used it either.

One last image: I see him from behind, standing at the gate in the wooden fence that bordered the road, the left half open. He's leaning his right elbow on the mailbox attached to the side that's closed. I think he's waiting for the postman.

Behind him is what we called the front garden (the kitchen garden was on the other side of the house), a tiny landscape garden with miniature lawns, shrubs—deutzia, weigela, rhododendron—and robinia, bay palms, or Japanese privet instead of tall trees, not forgetting the two indispensable chamaerops palms that survived bombing, fire, and demolition. All this, planted from seed or cuttings by Sergeant Perrier of the coast guard, my grandmother's father, seemed to us gigantic.

In front of him is "Kerangoff plain," a vast unfenced training ground where marines on maneuvers occasionally played at war games; the rest of the time the plain was deserted, left to us for our excursions and mushroom picking, and not least to the herd of sheep that kept the grass cropped, whose black droppings we collected for the rosebushes and potatoes.

And beyond lies the whole Rade de Brest, which you could see clearly from that height, from the mouth of the Elorn right up to the channel, with the naval dockyard in the foreground and the sheltered berths protected by two long causeways; the yawning gap—one red light, one green—right opposite our house seemed to be a magnificent extension of the latticed garden gate and the three granite steps leading to the corridor, long since gone, that divided the ground floor of the house into two equal parts. The front door, with its high rectangular judas window covered by a very elaborate wrought-iron grille, is now to be found, hardly changed, in New York, city of crime and rape, at the beginning of *Projet pour une révolution*. . . . Forgive me, Jean Ricardou.

And what's become of my grandfather, with his pale eyes lost on the gray horizon, bounded on the other shore of the harbor by the Crozon Peninsula and Menez-Hom? Perhaps that's him, old King Boris, still accompanied by the muffled thuds that echo from floor to floor, cellar to attic, the man who is taking such pains to repair the sliver of veneer chipped from his desk, before facing the firing squad with a smile of farewell. And yet the rooks in the bare hundred-year-old ash trees are without a doubt the ones from Le Mesnil.

A few short years after his death came the superb summer of 1940. I had just done brilliantly in my math course at the Brest lycée. The fine fleet had left the harbor at nightfall, never to return. On departing, the naval engineers had set fire to the underground reservoirs, which we then realized actually did exist. The fuel burned for almost a week. Amidst the din of explosions, burning pitch poured out of the hills near the Maison Blanche, drowning streams and meadows, while formidable columns of red flame and black smoke descended on the garden in hot, suffocating fumes thick with heavy soot, like snowflakes, and permeated with the acrid stench of a smoking kerosene lamp—the taste of defeat, along with the paradoxical sense of freedom you feel at the collapse of your own nation (psych. trap to be continued).

I described this sensation of awesome catastrophe and emptiness a few months later in my first prose work, which came after two or three poems written that year. It was a short story to be called "Comoedia," done in strict classical form for an amateur competition organized by a weekly newspaper that came out at the beginning of the Occupation. I never received a reply, and I too have lost the text. As I remember, it was of no interest: a sketchy adolescent love story ending obscurely in ruin.

The setting for the flirtation was probably inspired by my math class, which was coeducational, a fact that doubtless occupied my studious mind unconsciously during the school year. Anyway, my young hero, abandoned and crushed, saw the failure of his love affair counterpointed by our military defeat and disarmament. He finally embarked on one of those old tubs that carried a few reckless boys off to adventure, in search of the English coast—very few, actually, because of the deep-rooted hatred between these two peoples with rival navies, a hatred further exacerbated by very recent resentment over the common debacle, and felt strongly by my whole family. So the amorous disappointment bore no similarity to my own personal history, which was without obvious passion, nor to the dramatic departure when the reservoirs went up in flames. Or maybe it is my own ghost fleeing Vesuvius in pursuit of an indifferent, haughty Gradiva.

On the fifth day of the catastrophe I saw my first German soldier. He came rattling along on a motorcycle with a sidecar, up the sunken lane that led from the arsenal to the Kerangoff plain. A second soldier huddled in the passenger space, wearing the same heavy helmet that crushed the nape of his neck, and pointing a machine gun in front of him. Their faces were tired and drawn, livid with dust. Exactly the same greenish mineral color as their far from spectacular machine, they went diagonally across the plain toward the cemetery at Recouvrance, jolting over the uneven ground, solitary, ridiculous: our conquerors. . . . Today they can be seen again in *Labyrinthe* (*In the Labyrinth*), dead tired in their

archaic vehicle, vanguard of the enemy army that be-
sieged the captured city.

I left the house two months later to go back to Paris.
The next time I saw it, it was in ruins. Kerangoff plain no
longer exists. The uneven, winding road has been replaced by a straight blacktop street with sidewalks,
named after a field marshal of the previous war against
Germany, the one my father won; his stories of hero-
ism punctuating that interminable nightmare of mud
haunted the Parisian half of my overimaginative childhood with a nebulous fear (you'll be a soldier too). The
house, my birthplace, which my mother lovingly rebuilt
(this time in stone) around the old staircase that had
miraculously survived the bombing, is now hidden by
housing projects, and from the bedroom windows on
the first floor you can no longer greet the old ocean of
crystal waves haloed in gray mist.

Meanwhile, I'd gradually had to face my ambivalence
toward this sea I'd at first thought I was so estranged
from. In the end I am in fact bound to it by the strongest
of links: I felt myself inexorably drawn into the dreams
and darkness that disturb the depths beneath the apparent surface calm, as beneath the far too joyful fury of the
waves that break and drop back, sparkling like fireworks. For the whole period of the Occupation the
German military command forbade access to the Brittany coast; in their eyes, owning a family house was not
sufficient reason to go there. Perhaps I needed the physical break, the cutting of the umbilical cord, the long
separation, for the metamorphosis to take place in my
head.

I can also think of a possible intermediary: music,
which may have been a decisive contributing factor or
may at least have acted as a significant catalyst. At the
time I was discovering Wagner and Debussy. The indefi-

nite series of vague chords never coming to rest in a set tonality, never gaining a foothold, was like the tide rising wave after wave despite its deceptive ebb. I don't remember any sudden, dramatic revelation behind some pillar at the opera or in the Salle Pleyel, but I know that from the beginning of the forties I couldn't listen to *Pelléas* or *Tristan* without feeling instantly uplifted by the insidious, perilous surge of the sea, then sucked reluctantly into the heart of an unknown, unstable, irrational liquid universe ready to engulf me, its ineffable face at once the face of death and of desire: tenacious old illusion of our Western world from Plato to Hegel, even to Heidegger, permeating the whole Christian tradition too, for which this world is merely an appearance hiding another, more "real" world, which will only be lived after the final, blissful death by drowning.

When I do begin writing a novel, four years after the Liberation, I'm certainly not working from this perspective; on the contrary, my writing is a reaction against the fatal temptation to take annihilation for ultimate bliss, loss of consciousness for illumination, despair for beauty of soul. In all my early books I even led the fight with such persuasive valor, strengthening my fortifications with some polemical articles on theory, that in looking at the reviews from that time—unfavorable or otherwise—it's hard to find the slightest trace of the monsters I was combating. There was, of course, Maurice Blanchot, and a few more. But what about the others, all the others?

It's strange, though, that so many readers, not all of them lacking in sensitivity and intelligence, were so easily taken in. If I open *Le Voyeur* or *La Jalousie* today, what strikes me right away is precisely the strenuous, unflagging combat waged by the narrative voice, by Mathias the traveling salesman and the anonymous

27

husband as they struggle against the delirium lying in wait for them, which surfaces in many a turn of phrase and more than once takes over a whole paragraph. Obviously (and the same goes for me too, alas, when I read others) it's extremely difficult to perceive the complexity of a writer's text whenever it's the slightest bit devious. I make an exception of Roland Barthes, who is a past master in matters of guile. Grappling with his personal demons, he did his best to outwit them by searching for a "writing degree zero" in which he never believed. My so-called neutrality—mere protective clothing—came at just the right moment to fuel his discourse. And so I was dubbed an "objective novelist," or worse still, one who was attempting to be so, without an ounce of talent, and merely succeeded in being dull.

By chance yesterday, in the office that's been assigned to me for a few months at New York University, I came across a vigorously annotated copy of *Le Voyeur*, left on the littered bookshelves by one of my predecessors, who must have taught the book and hated it. Every time a particularly obvious trap is set he falls right into it and triumphantly notes in the margin the mistake I've made in relation to my detestable system. How can this professor fail to see that Mathias, deliberately contradicting everything I may have said about the honest use of grammatical tenses, undertakes to describe his days on the island in the third person and in the highly suspect past historic—which should be all the more suspicious in that he suddenly sees himself thwarted at key points in the narrative by short passages in the present tense that seem to escape his control. . . . But good heavens, not mine! At least give me that. Mathias—or more accurately, the text that "expresses" him—uses the traditional language of irrefutable truth precisely because he is hiding something: the gap in his timetable. Similarly, he gives a minute, geometrical description of the world around him, whose treachery he fears, *for the purpose of* neutralizing it. Moreover, the sea monster (the one that devours little girls) is explicitly present in the pages of the book, toward the end, and almost instantly you realize that Mathias, on the point of fainting, has just then lost his grip.

As for the absent narrator of *La Jalousie*, he is himself the blind spot, as it were, in a text based on the things that his gaze desperately tries to put in order, to control, so as to combat the conspiracy that constantly threatens to upset the tenuous fabric of his "colonialism": the luxuriant tropical vegetation, the rapacious sexuality attributed to the Blacks, the fathomless gaze of his own wife, and a whole parallel, indescribable universe made up of the noises surrounding the house. How is it that so little has been said about the role of hearing in this novel, which is even alleged to be devoted to one single sense, sight? The reason must lie, at least in part, in the disconcerting technique of the "empty center," which was beginning to develop in *Les Gommes* (*The Erasers*), and to which we'll have to come back.

But a more general question arises, for the author this time. Why complicate the reading of a novel with so many pitfalls and snares? That is, why *must* the text be set with traps? And how do these traps work? What is this strange relation I have with my indispensable reader, since I do my best to mislead and then baffle him? It's certainly not an easy question to answer, but I must try or we won't be able to go on.

Actually I am hounded on all sides: Why don't you say things more simply, why aren't you more accessible to the public, why don't you make an effort to be more comprehensible, etc.? But these are absurd ways of formulating the problem. I write first of all against myself, as we've already seen, and therefore against the public too. Make what more comprehensible? If I'm pursuing an enigma that appears to me as a lack in my own meaningful continuity, how could I possibly give a full, unbroken account of it? How could I express such a paradoxical relation to the world and to my own being "simply," a relation in which everything is ambiguous, contradictory, fleeting?

"Articulated" language, I emphasize again, is structured like our lucid consciousness, which is to say, according to the laws of meaning. Thus, it follows directly that it is incapable of accounting either for an external world that is precisely not us or for the restless ghosts within us. But at the same time I do have to use this material, language, however ill-suited it may be, because it is this lucid consciousness—and nothing else—that finds fault with non-sense and gaps.

I've already pointed out how the modern novel, in order to get beyond this (basic) contradiction, chooses to take it not as a subject of study but as the organizing principle of fiction. Let's take this further now. Bringing a fundamental lack into play in this way, through the very structure of the narrative, will immediately frustrate the reader, lure him in and then deceive him, show him his place in the text while simultaneously excluding him from it, trick him like those decoys whose mechanisms are most complex when their purpose is to produce nothing—no external object, no feeling; all they have to do is "function" like a peculiarly transparent multipurpose trap: trap for a humanist reading, for a politico-Marxist or Freudian reading, etc., and finally, trap for the enthusiast of structures with no meaning.

This is where Mallarmé's *Sonnet en x* meets Marcel Duchamp's *Grand Verre*, whose function is not to powder chocolate—external object—nor to crush the dark bachelor demons. Actually, what has just been said about written fiction applies to all the other constructions of contemporary art, although they aren't dependent on articulated language, from Jasper Johns's paintings to the silent theatrical performances of Bob

Wilson or Richard Foreman. The same applies *a fortiori* to the cinema, since it is an acknowledged medium of fiction. But perhaps words remain, after all, the privileged means of expressing an experience of the void—because they are more shocking in the eyes of the law. Is this, O Socrates, what the vulgar call gratuitousness? Let's examine this opinion, inherited from Sainte-Beuve. To begin with, we must be wary of those who use the word "gratuitous" as an insult. When I read in the paper that in such and such a film there are gratuitous tracking shots, I know it only means that people can't see their precise "signification." Gratuitousness, according to this consumer ideology, is apparently defined in opposition to the "surplus value" of meaning—which actually puts it on my side. And yet . . .

And yet, can't people see that I myself am constantly attempting to justify myself—as I am once again in these pages? Because I too have this ideological relation to meaning (to the law), this thirst to encompass meaning, this anxiety to supply it—of course I do. No, *Le Grand Verre* is not gratuitous, nor is *Sonnet en x*; if they were, they would yet again be on the side of sacrosanct simplicity and not restless research. Hence the increasing complication of my own constructions, with *Topologie d'une cité fantôme* and *Projet pour une révolution*, where anyone, by the way, could have spotted the famous bride stripped bare. . . . But let's not get ahead of ourselves, as King Menelaus would say.

So in 1948 I decide to write a novel. On the spur of the moment, I leave the Institut National de la Statistique, where I already had a career marked out for me, and retreat to my sister's in Bois-Boudran, Seine-et-Marne, to a biology laboratory in the depths of the country, a center for artificial insemination and hormone research.

My daily work—approximately forty minutes three times a day—consists in taking vaginal smears every eight hours from hundreds of sterile rats injected with urine from mares in foal, thus establishing their folliculin levels, the reaction threshold of each animal having previously been gauged with standard testing solutions. The rest of the time I spend writing *Un Régicide* on the back of pedigrees of Dutch bulls whose sperm we sell to the peasants. First I write down the title, then the quotation from Kierkegaard about the seducer who "goes through life leaving no trace behind"; with these first words the paradox is stated in the form of a self-contradictory object: the supreme crime that simultaneously effaces its own inscription. And the sea appears, my own double wiping out my footprints; then I write my opening sentence, eternal repetition of an action always already done, accomplished, without ever leaving a trace behind me: "Once again, at nightfall on the seashore, a stretch of fine sand broken by rocks and hollows has to be negotiated, sometimes with the water waist-deep. The sea is rising . . ." Insidious perils, fear, are keeping their appointment, as usual.

I'm absolutely sure that this opening is directly inspired by a recurring nightmare I had for months on end when I was an adolescent. A few pages later, the hero of the book, Boris the regicide (in this text it's the king who's called Jean, an onomastic situation reversed, after nine novels, in *Souvenirs du triangle d'or*), Boris the bachelor, Boris the dreamer, is grappling with feelings of hopelessness, ineptitude, and bewilderment, which he experiences in his molars, tongue, gums, and is trying at once to pinpoint, describe, and get rid of—which come to the same thing. Here again childhood anxieties are rising to the surface, just when the ghosts of my sexual deviation have reappeared in my life, in a more imperious manner than ever. Of course I'd been living with them for a long time, fifteen years, but now I have to accept the fact that only "perverse" scenes (or fantasies) excite me, which is all the more problematic since I am especially attracted to very young girls.

In this first novel the ocean and its uncertain shores appear in a narrative in the first-person present. The reader catches glimpses of them as if drifting through a dream (in which the plethora of metaphors almost drowns the "poetry" of the gray heathlands and the fog), a dream that breaks up and soon distorts a "realist" continuity written in the third-person past historic. Boris works in a huge factory that I have no difficulty recognizing as the Maschinenfabrik-Augsburg-Nürnberg (M.A.N.), where I myself learned to be a lathe operator during the war.

The enormous machine shop with its seemingly endless rows of automatic lathes and milling machines lined up as far as the eye can see in a bluish spray of oily emulsion that smells of burning grease; warehouses, their blind walls built of small, grimy bricks; the imposing entrance gate opening onto the long, straight, sad suburban avenue where ancient trams rattle along toward the distant cemetery in the south (we took the tram—as they called it in Brest—at the main station, where from dawn onward we got off trains covered in coal dust, packed with passengers who were more or less deportees, sleeping on two-tier bunks in wooden barracks that formed vast camps in the middle of the neighboring pine forests); and then the time clocks on the wall with the slots containing our cards, the metallic passes that have to be shown at every checkpoint—this whole scene, hardly changed, is the scene of my life in Nuremberg. On a roofbeam above me, painted in huge letters, was this harsh slogan, which also applied to the German workers: *Du bist eine Nummer und diese Nummer ist nul* ("You are a number and that number is zero").

Perhaps at first my regicide is rebelling against this unacceptable law: the surest way to be recognized as an individual is to commit the heinous political crime of killing the king. Although Boris in his factory has a job

more like my next one—statistician—in this first book
the sinister face of the established order comes from my
German experience, and today I realize this is no mere
coincidence. Disintegration, the inconceivable horror at
the heart of what had been the popular ideal proclaimed
by National Socialism (work, fatherland, sports, social
laws, the cult of nature, blond adolescents marching
along singing, a smile on their faces, bright-eyed and
innocent, soul as pure as body according to the most
reassuring imagery of cheerful good health)—I think
the brutal inversion of all these signs, which suddenly
revealed their other face, had a more profound effect on
me than the defeat of our own army five years earlier.

Of course, I experienced these two successive break-
downs very differently, but it isn't exactly in good taste
to admit it. The defeat of 1940 was certainly the defeat of
liberty, but my family said it was rather the overthrow of
levity, licence, negligence, and a weak, pleasure-
seeking mentality—in short, the defeat of the Third
Republic. The collapse of the Third Reich, on the contrary, was the collapse of a particular idea of order that
might have appeared awe-inspiring, the failure of a rig-
orous system that had become totalitarian, a collapse
into blood and madness. I have mentioned that my
parents were right-wing; I must explain this more fully.

According to the official version of the truth, which in
other climes sends historians off to die in penal servi-
.tude, those whose evil genius impels them to ask how
the battleship *Aurora* could have fired on the Winter
Palace when it wasn't in Leningrad during those glorious October days, whereas we are shown it well and
truly moored at the quay on the Neva facing the palace,
just where it should be, and freshly painted every year
(the truth has to be touched up regularly or it will
flake)—according, then, to the official discourse, France

at first appeared, at the Liberation, as a nation of heros pitted against the Occupation forces from the armistice onward in near unanimous resistance, a somewhat untenable position that could nevertheless be maintained for more than ten years without provoking outright laughter or too violent a protest. Then comes a complete turnaround: France was nothing but a pack of cowards and traitors that sold its soul and the whole of the Jewish people for a single crust of black bread.

I'm not going to venture a third version (I'm not a historian, thank God). But I must make it clear at this point in my modest autobiography that my experience hardly corresponds to either of those images. Let there be no misunderstanding: it's merely a question of saying, of trying to say, how I saw things around me, or even more subjectively, how I imagine today that I saw things then.

I was a good son, the very opposite of a rebel. I got along fine at home, and as soon as I got back there, I would recount in detail everything I'd seen and done at school or on the way. As for values, I had no trouble accepting most of my parents' political or moral options: it's wicked to tell lies, take the world as you find it, don't cheat on exams, the Popular Front is leading France to wrack and ruin, if you work hard your material and spiritual welfare will be assured, etc., or even "The richest aren't the poorest," since our folklore comprised numerous meaningless aphorisms, almost as a way of sending up those we did believe in.

I probably didn't have an unquestioning, unreserved admiration for my good parents, but I did feel a sort of sacred alliance with them, a fraternal community, a staunch solidarity. My father, mother, sister, and I formed a sort of clan. For more than fifteen years I even wore a ring, a kind of talisman, made of four intertwined aluminum bands that I'd picked out of a box of spare parts at the M.A.N. factory in 1943. Such family loyalty inevitably resulted in a certain alienation from the rest of mankind: a vague feeling of superiority, or at least difference.

One day at my primary school on Rue Boulard, I had proudly replied to a schoolmate who was boasting about the captain's stripes his father had won in the service that mine was a lieutenant colonel. When I got home I asked for more information about the military hierarchy. In fact, as a pupil at Arts et Métiers in Cluny, my father, in a spirit of anarchy, had refused the additional military training that would have enabled him to serve as an officer. Mobilized on leaving school in August 1914 and sent to the front as an ordinary soldier, he spent four years in action and finished the war in the hospital "with serious facial injuries," decorated with the Médaille Militaire, the Croix de Guerre, palms and citations, but only a second lieutenant.

Antimilitarism has certainly been one of the constants in his impassioned existence—this curious right-wing man who would show his children, not without a certain pride, the remark in red on his report card from Arts et Métiers (where at the beginning of this century they still wore uniforms and close-cropped hair): "Affects a singularly untidy and slovenly appearance." And so, that evening at the family table, where he invariably had his garlic sausage and *café au lait*, I learned that he was only a second lieutenant at the end of hostilities, and then a lieutenant as an engineer with the French occupation troops in the repossessed factories of Lorraine, but that if I wanted to, I could give him the five stripes of a colonel or the simple insignia of a sergeant, since these things were of no importance. Such was the clan's pride that it had no need of stripes.

The only war spoils he'd brought back were the complete works of Schiller—a large tome bound in gray cloth and printed in Gothic type, of course—and a German flare gun, a sort of enormous pistol with a spectacular hammer, almost as heavy as a rifle, with a short barrel as thick as my child's arm. This impressive trophy was hung out of reach on the wall of the room we called the "study," which was used as the children's room. Except as a special favor, we were forbidden to play with this harmless weapon, since you could easily crush a finger under the hammer or if you were careless when handling the well-oiled breech.

After his evening coffee, Papa would sit at the desk (a piece of furniture resembling a chest of drawers, from American surplus) and enthusiastically translate Schiller's plays, one after the other, conscientiously covering squared exercise books with minute writing in indelible pencil. I think it was a sort of literal yet quite free translation, since this zealous amateur didn't use his dictionary as often as he might, and most of the grammar must have been beyond him. Guessing, improvising, not bothered if his text didn't make sense or sounded strange, he progressed quite quickly, unconcerned about other peoples' opinions. Anne-Lise, my sister, whom we used to call Nanette, claims that it was one of the traumas of her youth (as when she realized a few years before that there was no Father Christmas) when she discovered that our father didn't know a word of German, that he hadn't learned it at school or anywhere else.

Were we poor? It's obviously relative. Anyway, as a child I never felt in the least bit poor. I never thought of comparing such and such a schoolmate's apartment (after primary school I won a scholarship to Lycée Buffon, and my sister was a scholarship student too, at Lycée Victor-Duruy), or the apartment of one of my mother's few friends (like that close friend who was a dentist in Brest), with the three cramped rooms on Rue Gassendi where all four of us were still living when I was over twenty; we didn't have carpets or chandeliers, and the three bare bulbs hanging from the ceiling on little brass fixtures seemed perfectly normal to me, as did the sofa bed we unfolded at night to change the dining room into a bedroom once my sister, as modesty required, stopped sleeping in the same room as me.

My father, thanks to his soldier's pension, didn't make use of his engineering diploma from Arts et Métiers to go into the metallurgical business; instead he joined a brother-in-law, who was a bit better off, to found the Société Industrielle du Cartonnage, a pompous trade name for a tiny factory that made cardboard boxes for mass-produced dolls. Three or four workers assembled the boxes, my uncle delivered them, but my father had the hardest job: all day long he fed large sheets of brownish cardboard through the circular guillotine—a dangerous job that should have been done by a qualified worker; sadly, the cost of the wages was incompatible with the prospective and ever uncertain profits of the business.

On Saturday nights, sitting at his desk, which for once had been cleared of Schiller, my worried father initialed with a huge, illegible, superb flourish never-ending bundles of bills, repeatedly carried forward, many of which—I found out later—were purely and simply accommodation bills. I have since realized that throughout our childhood he lived in a state of permanent anxiety about this endless bookkeeping. And I can still see his fingertips, strangely smooth and red, so worn from being rubbed by the cardboard that in the cold winters (the workshop wasn't heated) open cuts took weeks to heal.

But on Sunday mornings he would resole the family shoes while singing tunes from operettas, cheerfully mangling words and music. He had all kinds of tools piled up in the cramped kitchen, including a child's workbench that Father Christmas had left for me in front of our parents' black marble fireplace, where toys always appeared on the twenty-fifth of December—in this case a toy that was certainly much larger than the chimney, and one I still use occasionally in my more spacious home in Le Mesnil. Watching my father at work, I developed a taste for manual jobs, from carpentry to reinforced concrete, and I'm sorry that I no longer have enough time to restore all the masonry, door frames, and loose iron fittings at the property I love.

When the shoes were repaired, Papa took us for long springtime walks along the fortifications toward Montrouge, which was almost like being in the country. There was new grass, there were lilacs around the huts, and in the most desolate places bright yellow coltsfoot shot up through the whitish clay (the big leaves that came later were dried and used as a tobacco substitute during the Occupation). About four in the afternoon we would come home for dinner, which Maman had cooked while we were out; we invariably had, one week out of two, roast chicken or leg of lamb with fried potatoes and salad. The lovely smell permeated the whole apartment. We were hungry. Night fell swiftly, mauve-gray outside, and the electric light on the round table where the clan was gathered shed a warm orange glow as we told Maman about our day's adventures.

I have nothing but happy memories of those Sundays children are usually supposed to hate. And yet I think back on them without nostalgia: I don't feel that my way of life or my relations with the world have changed fundamentally; as for the present narrative, which I work on day after day, against myself, I wonder if it's so different from the painstaking, inaccurate, absurd translation of Schiller's complete works. For dessert Papa would read us (rather badly) particularly polemical, vitriolic extracts from the latest article by Daudet or Maurras, often including obscene jokes against republican institutions and their official representatives. I don't know what the extreme right-wing press is like today, but I do remember L'Action française in the thirties as a well-written, exuberant paper, much taken with Greco-Latin culture. The most violently offensive attacks were usually couched in the language of Cicero.

From my two left-wing grandfathers, staunch republicans of a confirmed yet good-humored secular turn of mind, Dreyfusards, always ready to denounce the sinister union of the army and the church, my parents had retained an almost visceral atheism. The pernicious part played on every level by the Roman Catholic church was as little to be doubted as the fundamental incompetence of the generals. If the excommunication of Action Française—engineered, it was said, by Aristide Briand (nicknamed from then on "the blessed pimp")—upset many Christians, for us it was merely additional proof of the justice of the cause. Advocates of state Catholicism (for the people) yet excommunicated by the pope, monarchists yet disowned by the pretender to the throne, the A.F. leaders perfectly suited this family, which liked nothing better than to feel it was different. Contempt for the orthodox, a horror of the herd (the *servum pecus*), plus the ludicrous series of parliamentary coalitions— all this led naturally to a pronounced hatred of democracy.

After the ritual Sunday meal, Papa would sleep or go play a game of manille with the Jura cousins, concierges in Belleville. And then there were the special Sundays. When the large canal at Versailles froze over, we would skate on ice lit by the winter sun. Sticking to the old country custom, we had detachable skates fastened to heavy walking shoes by a system of clamps. We took the train. We wore knitted scarves wrapped around our necks. At nightfall, on our way back, we bought bags of hot chestnuts roasted on street corners in big black iron stoves enveloped in fragrant blue smoke. This was a great joy. One night when it had snowed a lot, Papa had a sudden impulse and made us rudimentary (straight) skis out of small planks and leather straps so he could take us to glide over the slopes in Montsouris park the next morning. . . . And then it's night once more, and the lights come on in the peaceful dusk frozen in the frost.

These sensations associated with night falling early in the wintry city, or just after the beginning of the school year, toward the end of autumn, when the lights are already coming on earlier in the shabby windows of the neighborhood bakeries or groceries, while it's still fairly mild and a fine drizzle sprinkles gleaming light onto the unevenly paved streets, between charcoal-gray sidewalks where the last decaying leaves of the plane trees cling, musky and glistening . . . I've often mentioned these very vivid (yet peaceful) sensations—of evening calm, welcoming lamps, the distant hum of the city, vegetable soup, scorched paper shades—as perhaps the main reasons that impelled me to write a novel. To write because of the color yellow noticed on an old wall: I know exactly what that means. Faced with the aggressive harshness of a book like *La Jalousie*, do my readers have the right to be surprised at such a confession? I think not.

These extremely strong impressions, unforgettable although vague and fleeting, provoked by the sticky (often comforting) adjectivity of the familiar world, by its soon unbearable emotional charge, by its ambiguous insistence—these are what compel us to undertake its description, to explore it or give it form. But certainly with no intention of reproducing that adjectivity. Quite the contrary, in my own case. And yet any sensitive reader would have no trouble recognizing in the "childhood memories" of Wallas, the troubled hero of *Les Gommes*, or in the two plaintive notes borrowed by the New York firemen from Parisian firemen in *Projet pour une révolution*, the faint echo of such poignant emotions . . .

41

Now that I've taken up the present narrative again, in October of 1983 (as I indicated in the two pages added at the beginning of this volume), in the middle of the vast, foreign, rugged plains of Alberta, Edmonton, a city of luxurious modern skyscrapers totally different from the old neighborhood, the fourteenth arrondissement, between the Montparnasse cemetery and the Porte d'Orléans, I read over those lines about my family life around 1930 and am again amazed. Once more I wonder what these evocations mean. Why spend so much time recounting these more or less pointless anecdotes? When they do seem at all meaningful to me, I instantly blame myself for choosing them (putting them together, maybe fabricating them) precisely in order to give them a meaning. If on the contrary they're merely stray fragments that have come adrift, whose potential significance I myself may be looking for, why did I pick only these out of the hundreds and thousands that come up at random?

I'm caught in a bind: either I'm elucidating prefabricated meanings or, on the other hand, exploiting the gratuitousness of a purely random pointillism (illusory into the bargain) as I grope my way forward at the mercy of obvious or absurd associations. If only I could hope to rediscover as I go along (by what miracle?) a few of the key moments that have formed me. But are there such things? And here the idea of a hierarchy, of classification, comes up again. "Tell me how you classify," Barthes proposed, "and I'll tell you who you are." A refusal to classify, then, would constitute a refusal to be, a willingness merely to exist. Then why write?

Of course, a considerable filial affection appears in my clan hagiography, like a small bouquet left on a grave. My father and mother lived mainly for their children; the best part of their work, worries, plans involved us. Isn't this a poor return in comparison? Am I not merely sketching a picturesque father, and doesn't everyone seem picturesque when painted? Can we accept that the entire life of a man leaves only these meager traces, forgotten at the back of a drawer with a few yellowing photos of his irregular features, his big moustache, his puttees?

They are probably still there: the thousands of letters he wrote my mother every day, over more than fifty years—love letters—even when there was a postal strike, whenever they were apart (for instance, when she was in Brest with us for the summer vacation). There must be bundles of them in chronological order lying at the bottom of some worm-eaten trunk in the attic at Kerangoff. Even at the time they were hard to decipher, and doubtless they too will crumble into dust as soon as they're disturbed.

As for the obvious pleasure it gave me such a short time ago to say that our father wasn't left-wing, it seems that this is rapidly turning out to be less scandalous than I thought. Who could it shock today? Now that the "socialists" are in power in France, all unorthodox intellectuals will soon find themselves back on the right, after a short purgatorial silence.

Another problem arises, from the fact that I'm also talking about myself. Or even: solely about myself, as usual. My parents—that's already me taking shape. For whoever's interested, I affirm my objection to the autobiography that claims to assemble a whole life (as if it could ever be watertight), making it into a closed book with no gaps or smudges, like those old field marshals who convincingly recast their ancient battles (won at cost, or lost) for future generations. Now this downward path, this precipice I'm so close to, is a constant threat. An awareness of the dangers isn't sufficient proof against temptation.

In the Museum of Modern Art in New York, there's been a huge canvas on display for some weeks, where I can be seen (as the title confirms) surrounded by scattered fragments. The young artist (whose name has slipped my mind)* has painted me kneeling in the middle of a sort of vast desert strewn with pieces of rubble that I'm in the process of cleaning, one by one, with a brush and washbasin. If you look more closely, you can see that they're in fact perfectly recognizable objects, although they're fossilized, smashed to pieces—the wreckage of our civilization, culture, and history, such as the Sphinx at Giza, Frankenstein's face, or some infantrymen from the First World War—mixed up with disjointed fragments from my own writings, novels, or films (for example, Françoise Brion in *L'Immortelle*), and even my own face and a miniature version of me on my knees cleaning, turned to stone like everything else.

I recognize myself in this very witty allegory with pleasure. But having carefully cleaned the pieces, am I not now artfully putting them in order? Perhaps even sticking them back together again to shape a destiny, a statue, the little boy's terrors and joys forming a solid base for the themes or techniques of the future writer.

To put things in order. Once and for all! The old naive obsession resurfaces here and there, ironic, insistent, hopeless, throughout my entire work as a novelist, where the many-sided hero never stops going over his daily routine with its flimsy framework, counts and recounts his banana trees, conscientiously masters his anguish, or goes over the same episode again and again (hoping each time to arrive at a logical, rational conclusion), for example, the precise account of what he saw and did at the Blue Villa on the evening in question. We must also note the minor characters who are partly

---

* This American painter of the neofigurative school is Mark Tansey, and the painting is *Robbe-Grillet Cleansing Every Object in Sight.*—Ed.

conscious of this senseless obstinacy, such as Garinati, the clumsy murderer, lining up the objects on his mantelpiece, Lady Ava trying one last time to put her papers in order before she dies, or the prisoner in *Triangle d'or*, who undertakes an exhaustive description of the bare walls of his cell "to vindicate himself" of who knows what crime.

Soon after the manuscript of *Les Gommes* was accepted by Editions de Minuit, having spent the modest sum I'd scrupulously saved during my far too brief stay in the colonies, I found a convenient little job in Paris thanks to my qualifications as an agronomist and to the help of Jean Piel, who was then inspector general of the Economie Nationale, Georges Bataille's brother-in-law, and de facto director of the prestigious review *Critique*, in which my first jottings were published. So I was working at the Assemblée Permanente des Présidents de Chambres d'Agriculture on Rue Scribe, where I shared a huge office with two colleagues who must have been legal experts. My table adjoined that of a remarkably thin, severe man who sat opposite. He looked at me, over the files and heaps of documents that I tried in vain to pile up as a screen, with the silent disapproval of the just man who has detected an impostor at first glance.

He was only there for a week or a bit longer, and yet I have retained a surprisingly clear, solid image of this phantom judge, with whom I hadn't exchanged ten sentences. He must have been seriously ill, was certainly aware of it, and knew he was going to die. One morning, on arriving, he began to take an inventory of his drawers. For three whole days I watched him, always silent, two meters away from me, sorting out masses of business letters, technical documents, minutes of meetings, rough drafts, tables of figures, press clippings, and various odd bits of paper, rereading them, tearing some up, annotating others for his successor, and filing in carefully labeled folders everything he thought ought to survive him. Then he left the office punctually. He went into the hospital that same evening for hopeless surgery and died the next day on the operating table.

I had read his condemnation of me in his dark-ringed, sunken eyes, which were already remote, their mournful glitter seeming to come from very far away: from the other side of the grave, I thought later, with no exaggeration. Of course he had instantly realized I was correcting the proofs of a novel and not articles on agricultural economy. He had seen that my mind was elsewhere, that I too was merely passing through. I was a fake office employee. I had indeed been at the Agro (he had had to check it in a yearbook), but I was a fake agronomist. Although I didn't know it at the time, I was already a fake when I worked at the Institut des Fruits et Agrumes Coloniaux, where I'd gone to do research after finishing *Un Régicide*, three years before.

A regional manager who lived on another island in the Antilles had visited me in Fort-de-France while on an inspection tour; he had shown me a report published by one of our research stations in Africa. I conscientiously studied what had been done, the experimental methods, the meticulous account of problems that had arisen, the columns of measurements and the reservations about their statistical use, etc. The next day I pointed out to my superior that as all this research led to no concrete result whatsoever, the reports might just as well be considered imaginative exercises. I quite seriously offered to write a monthly report exactly like this one, in a few days and entirely on my own, using several pseudonyms if necessary . . .

He took me seriously too. But a few months later, when I was in the hospital in Guadeloupe with multiple tropical diseases confirmed by all kinds of examinations and tests, this honest and upright man, who was not lacking in shrewdness—and who did like me, I think, and could appreciate the qualities I had given proof of professionally, despite everything—unhesitatingly stated in his report to the head office in Paris, which was concerned about my health, that in his opinion, in my case, it was all "in the mind": an irrevocable judgment (yet probably not as unjust as I thought at the time) that can be found again seven years later in *La Jalousie*, concerning the colonial diseases undermining the health of the invisible Christiane, my boss having left some of his crudest characteristics (including that phrase) to the character Franck, the neighboring planter who always comes to dine without his excessively delicate wife.

In the last stage of his life Roland Barthes (him again) seemed obsessed with the idea that he was merely an impostor: that he had spoken of everything, from Marxism to linguistics, without really knowing anything. Already, many years before, I'd thought he was unduly affected by the criticisms of Picard, who vigorously denounced his misreading of the "real" Racine and his times. And yet Barthes had made it clear that all he was doing in his *Racine* was offering a contemporary reading, which was therefore subjective, risky, and precisely contexted. But he was suddenly chilled by the angry frown emanating from the old Sorbonne and felt a complex mixture of hatred and dread. And so, later, feeling his age, he became more and more troubled by the probable existence—which he suspected—of real seventeenth-century scholars, real teachers, real semiologists.

In vain I retorted that of course he was an impostor, precisely because he was a real *écrivain* (and not an *écrivant*, to use his own distinction), and that a writer's "truth" can only exist, if at all, in the accumulation, excess, and transcendence of his necessary lies. He would give his inimitable smile, a blend of unpretentious intelligence and friendship, but there was a certain distance, an absence from the world that was growing

47

more and more pronounced. He wasn't convinced: he told me that I certainly had the right to be an impostor, that it was even my duty, but not his, since he wasn't a creator. He was wrong. It is precisely his work as a scriptor that will last. The semidisrepute into which many people would like to see him fall so soon after his death is merely the result of a misunderstanding: the role of "thinker" that was foisted upon him.

Was Barthes a thinker? The question immediately raises another: What is a thinker today? Not so very long ago a thinker had to provide his fellow citizens with certainties, or at least with some rigid, consistent, inflexible straight lines that would underpin his own discourse and so guide the minds of his readers and the consciousness of his time. A thinker was an intellectual guru. Certainty was his essential characteristic, his official brief.

Roland Barthes was a slippery thinker. After his inaugural lecture at the Collège de France, I was expressing enthusiasm for his accomplished performance when a strange young girl turned on me, passionate and angry: "What are you admiring? He didn't say a thing from start to finish!" That wasn't quite accurate; he had indeed been saying something, yet he avoided pinning this "something" down: using the method he'd been perfecting for many years, he withdrew from what he was saying as he went along. Deliberately undermining his provocative statement that all speech is fascist, which had caused such a furor that evening, he gave a disturbing demonstration of a discourse that was not a discourse: one that destroyed in and of itself, step by step, any temptation to dogmatism. What I admired in that voice, which had just kept us in suspense for two whole hours, was precisely that it left my freedom intact, and more, strengthened it anew with each turn of phrase.

Dogmatism is nothing but the serene discourse of truth (complacent, solid, unequivocal). The traditional thinker was a man of truth, yet a short time ago he could still believe in all good faith that the reign of truth was advancing hand in hand—same goal, same battles, same enemies—with the progress of human liberty. On the pediment of a solid neo-Greek monument at the University of Halifax, in Nova Scotia, we read, "The truth guarantees your liberty"; and the letterhead I used in Edmonton this autumn has the following lofty motto: "*Quaecumque vera.*" Beautiful utopia, beautiful cheat that illumined the euphoric dawn of our bourgeois society, and one century later the dawn of scientific socialism. Alas, today we know where that science leads. Truth, in the final analysis, has always and only served oppression. Too many hopes, wretched disappointments, and blood-soaked paradises teach us in any case to be wary of it.

The preceding lines and those that follow were originally part of an article I was asked to write for *Le Nouvel Observateur* on the anniversary of Barthes's death, just before the presidential election in the spring of 1981. At this point in my text I made a joke, today out of date and somewhat bitter, which I nevertheless reproduce: "I'll vote for the Socialist Party candidate, since he at least hasn't got a platform."

Unfortunately we then saw the candidate in question, who'd become our monarch, turn around and take very seriously promises that many of his friends had until then seen only as vague speculations for electoral purposes, abstract ideas of the opposition, which would need to be completely revised when they were eventually put into practice. Nothing of the sort has happened: premature nationalization that has been needlessly disastrous, the dictatorial, uniform reduction of the work week, opposed by the unions themselves—the left's victory resulted instantly in a flood of shortsighted measures carried out in defiance of circumstances (as well as in defiance of the most experienced advisers), and solely justified, we are told, by the fact that they were "in the platform."

Certainly in all these decisions of principle, which weren't made in the national interest or in the interest of the people, the pledges that had to be given to the Communist allies must have weighed heavily: these allies, not the least of whose defects is obviously that they—they, at least—believe in truth, that is, in the absolute and definitive value of what was judged to be right, once and for all, sixty or more years ago. In any case, we have once more been able to gauge on this occasion how pernicious a platform can be as soon as it's taken as law.

And even if the problems of human liberty are not exactly the same in running a government and in the lawless pursuit of literature, which assuredly lacks sanctions besides, there may yet be an art common to these two so disparate powers: the ability to contradict oneself in order to move on. As for me, I will never side with those who reproach our president for having altered course a few months later, changed tack, as it were, right in the middle of the storm he had unleashed. On the contrary, I like to think that such a daring maneuver shows that there is still some flexibility at the heart of this nascent socialism, this too respectful heir of outmoded traditions. It is said that on the day of his fatal accident Roland Barthes had lunch with François Mitterrand. Let's hope that on leaving he convinced him of the radical virtues of pulling back, of reexamination, of continuous change.

For he is slippery as an eel (I'm talking about Barthes again), and his shifts are not simply the result of chance, nor do they stem from a weakness in judgment or a character flaw. "Messages" that change, branch off, veer in other directions—this is what he teaches. So it follows that our last "real" thinker will have been the one who preceded him: Jean-Paul Sartre. He still wanted to enclose the world in a total (totalitarian?) system worthy of Spinoza and Hegel. But at the same time Sartre was possessed by the modern idea of liberty, and that, thank God, is what undermined all his endeavors. His grand constructions—novels, criticism, or pure philosophy—have remained one after the other unfinished, open on all sides.

From the standpoint of his project, Sartre's work is a failure. However, it's this failure that interests and excites us today. Wanting to be the last philosopher, the last thinker in terms of totality, he ends up being a pioneer of the new structures of thought: uncertainty, mobility, the breaking of new ground. And we can now see that the statement of "useless passion" at the end of *L'Etre et le néant* (*Being and Nothingness*) wasn't so very different from Jean Paulhan's "Consider this unsaid," though they appeared to be poles apart.

In 1950 Barthes enters this intellectual arena, which already seems to be in ruins. Strangely, he is initially drawn to the reassuring work of Marx. In a quarrel with Albert Camus over *La Peste* (*The Plague*), he silenced the liberal humanist with the supremacy of "historical materialism," as if it were some absolute value. But soon, gradually, he withdrew from Marxism, without a fuss, tiptoeing as always.

He was once more lured by great systems of thought: psychoanalysis, linguistics, semiology. Hardly had the new label of semiologist had time to stick before he detested it. Openly ridiculing "our three policemen: Marx, Freud, Saussure," he ended by denouncing the intolerable imperialism of all rigid systems in his famous apologue of the frying pan: A "valid" system of thought that is too coherent is like boiling oil: whatever you put into it always comes out fried.

And yet Barthes's work is not a disavowal, because of the constantly renewed movement of the self outward, this movement that constitutes freedom (which could never become an institution, since it only exists at the moment of its own birth); this is precisely what he had been pursuing passionately from the outset, from Brecht to Bataille, from Racine to Proust to the New Novel, from dialectics to his analysis of fashion. And like Sartre before him, Barthes discovers very soon that the novel or the theater—more so than the essay—are the natural setting in which concrete freedom can be most violently and effectively acted out. Fiction is like philosophy's "world of becoming." Was Roland Barthes in his turn a novelist? The question instantly gives rise to another: What is a novel today?

Paradoxically, in the 1950s, using my own novels as infernal machines in his terrorist activities, he would attempt to reduce their cunning dislocations, their implicit phantoms, their autoerasures, their gaps, to a universe of things that would merely affirm its own objective, literal solidity. Of course that aspect was present in my books (and in my theoretical writings), but as one of two irreconcilable poles of a contradiction. Barthes chooses to ignore completely the monsters lurking in the shadows of the hyperrealist picture. And when the ghosts and specters in *L'Année dernière à Marienbad* (*Last Year at Marienbad*) invade the screen all too visibly, he beats a retreat.

I think he himself was grappling with analogous contradictions. He refused to see in *Les Gommes* or *Le Voyeur* the specter of *Oedipus Rex* or the obsession with sexual crime because, struggling with his own demons, he only needed my writing for its cleansing function. Like a good terrorist, he had only chosen one angle of the text, the most obviously acute, so he could use me in his thrust and parry. But in the evening, when he came down from the barricades, he would go home to wallow joyfully in Zola's rich prose thickened with adjectives

. . . even if he did later reproach the "adjectivity" of the snow in my *Labyrinthe*. Finally, ten years on, when *Projet pour une révolution à New York* appeared, he recovered his enthusiasm and praised it as a perfect yet "mobile" "Leibnizian model."

None of this answers the important question: What novels would he himself have written? He talked about this more and more, in public and in private. I don't know whether there are any rough drafts or fragments among his papers. In any case, I'm sure they wouldn't resemble either *Les Gommes* or *Projet*. He said that he could only write "real novels" and spoke of his problems with the past historic and the characters' proper names. In a shift even more dramatic than before, it seemed that the literary landscape around him had slid back to the end of the nineteenth century. . . . After all, why not? The meaning of any research must not be defined *a priori*. And Barthes was subtle and devious enough to transform this so-called real novel once more, into something new, baffling, unrecognizable.

Henri de Corinthe, at least his memory, seems (has always seemed?) still more elusive, more difficult to grasp, and often even suspect. Was he an impostor too, although of a different kind? Many of the people who knew him think so today, particularly those whose information and images are drawn solely from the gutter press. Anyway, it has to be admitted that his activities in Buenos Aires and Uruguay at the end of the Second World War and over the following decade are open to a multiplicity of interpretations. Trafficking in shady merchandise, girls, drugs, small arms (I must have used him more or less consciously as a model for Edouard Manneret in *La Maison de rendez-vous*, who also borrows—I think—the physique of Mallarmé at his worktable in the portrait by Manet), dealing in pictures too, fake or otherwise, high or low politics, espionage—all these may be valid hypotheses and are not necessarily incompatible. Moreover, one may wonder why this senior officer, who didn't seem to be in any particular danger, left France in such a hurry when the Americans entered Paris.

When I was a child I thought that Corinthe was a comrade of my father's from the trenches. Their friendship, which was otherwise inexplicable, could only have begun in the glorious mud of Cote 108 and Les Eparges. I realized some time later that this was impossible. My father was twenty in 1914, and Henri de Corinthe was much younger, certainly not old enough to take part in that war, not even as a volunteer on the eve of the armistice. My obstinate confusion about this important point was doubtless the result of the legendary aspect of this conflict—fabulous yet still recent—which had captured my imagination very early on, and which was simply called the Great War, as if to distinguish it in advance from all others, past and future.

Neither family stories, which were curiously underplayed (in order not to disturb our young minds unduly), nor the overrated books by people like Roland Dorgelès, nor the heavy albums published by L'Illustration, which we had on Rue Gassendi, reverently bound in fawn-colored leather and embossed in gold, with countless photos taken (more or less) from life indiscriminately mixed in with heroic prints in a realistic style, nor even the injury to his inner ear from which my father still suffered, managed to draw those cannons, cavalcades, corpses, that everlastingly muddy ground, that barbed wire, that victory, out of a past that was already too awesome, too formidable to belong to any domain but myth. Didn't Henri de Corinthe himself tower over the common herd like some legendary figure? His personal history, filled with grandeur, shrouded in disquieting mystery, instantly found its natural place in a setting so appropriate it seemed made for him.

It was in fact a quarter of a century later that he distinguished himself in battle, as a cavalry officer. But there probably was something anachronistic about that futile, bloody charge at the head of his dragoons, in June 1940, against the German armored divisions. So I can only imagine the sacrificed squadron as an old-fashioned, yellowing sepia print in L'Illustration. Lieutenant Colonel Corinthe (who anyway was only a major at the time of the German attack) is charging on his white horse, his sword drawn amidst the standards; oddly, he's looking toward the rear, doubtless to encourage his horsemen, whose gaudy uniforms and glittering helmets with streaming plumes are more reminiscent of some parade of the republican guard.

But in the foreground, on the far left of the picture, almost under the hooves of the nearest horses, one of which seems about to trample his body, is a wounded man—or rather, it is to be feared, a dying man. Half prostrate, the man is trying to raise himself on one elbow while his other arm—the right—stretches forward in the direction of his commanding officer and toward the smoke from the nearby enemy guns. There's no sword in his outstretched hand now, and howls of pain, not war cries, must be coming from his open mouth. And yet the parted lips under his fine-pointed moustache, the sweep of his arm, the very features of the soldier lying in the flower-strewn grass of June, down to the expression in his eyes—all these details are identical to those that draw us to the center of the composition: the handsome, resplendent officer on his white mount, its nostrils flaring. And at times it seems to me that the officer is looking down at the fallen dragoon, as if to bid farewell to his mortally wounded comrade, his double, his own life.

It is not particularly surprising that a few years later

this same Corinthe could be cast as a traitor, and then—in really confusing circumstances—as an assassin. An assassin or a traitor doesn't necessarily lack courage. More disturbing, certainly, is the hypothesis that his military feats were deliberately faked, or more precisely, "borrowed" from a school friend who disappeared without trace in the turmoil. Similar things are said about his courageous deeds in the Resistance, which are all the more difficult to verify in that they took place in a particularly troubled time and region, and the rare survivors are hardly willing to talk today about what they were doing when the area was liberated, an episode they are extremely reticent about. But if, as some say, Comte Henri did usurp the credit and glory of a real hero, his case is even more contemptible, since he may very well have had something to do with his disappearance.

It seems it's this Corinthe who inspired my split protagonist Boris Varissa/Jean Robin in the film *L'Homme qui ment*, for which I've often cited three more literary sources: the traditional Don Juan; the usurping tsar Boris Godunov, from Pushkin and Moussorgsky; and K., the ostensible land surveyor who attempts to besiege the castle in Kafka's novel.

Don Juan is the man who has chosen his own word, daring, capricious, and contradictory, as the unique foundation of his own—human—truth, a truth that can only exist in the present moment, as against God's Truth, which is by definition eternal. The moment—that's liberty. Don Juan knows this in his bones. And society condemns him precisely for being a libertine. He loves young women because they listen to him and so flesh out his discourse; it is they who finally create his tenuous reality. His killing of the father is like the killing of the king, that is, the ideological law claiming to be

56

God's law. A father willing to listen to him would straightaway cease to be the father. "There's no such thing as a good father," wrote Jean-Paul Sartre, who through self-hatred and hatred for his entire race deliberately yet misguidedly confused Papa, the good angel of the home, with the Pope, guardian angel of dogma.

Boris Godunov is the false father, the murderer. He had the last son of Ivan the Terrible, Tsarevitch Dmitri, whom he was supposed to protect, put to death so that he could become tsar in his place. He then reigns as absolute monarch. But he will be pursued all his life by a double incarnation of retribution whose mere presence leads him inexorably to madness and death: first the ghost of the murdered child who *returns* to demand reparation for the crime (God's truth, which is society's truth, can never be definitively abolished); and then, on the other hand, the more solid shape of a new impostor, Grigori the monk, who passes in the eyes of the credulous masses as Ivan's last son miraculously resurrected from the tomb. This false Dmitri, having gained the favor of a local princess in Poland, recruits an army of malcontents and ambitious men, soon joined by all the wretches in the empire. The last words Boris will utter as he dies in a fit of delirium are: "I am . . . still . . . tsar!" This is also the final cry of another mad emperor, Albert Camus's Caligula, as he falls under the knives of the conspirators: "I am still alive!" And it's doubtless what the wounded dragoon in the picture cried out before disappearing in the mud of Reichenfels under the hooves of the maddened horses of his hundred and twenty comrades-in-arms.

K.'s relations with the law are, as we know, more complex: he pretends to be more naive, innocent, as it were, when he's simply more devious. At first he pretends he's been called (as a surveyor, why not), whereas obviously nobody has asked anything of him. Then he's surprised that he's not welcomed with more ceremony. He complains, argues, negotiates. Like his brother Joseph in *The Trial*, he readily seduces the young girls he meets, whom he hopes to make his allies. He hangs on, stands his ground, protests, persists. He's undeterred when rebuffed. Gradually he creeps along all the back roads that might lead him to his goal, getting nearer and nearer to the forbidden door, which he knows very well cannot be entered, except by a corpse (who has lost his freedom in one blow). He always plays the victim, when it's he himself who is persecuting the "castle."

His strategy is guided by a sort of instinctive knowledge of everything connected with the law. This isn't surprising: he is not opposed to the law. He is the law and the criminal. His words—paradoxical, obstinate, unreasonable though seemingly reasonable—without which he would be nothing, are the very text of the book. If *L'Homme qui ment*, despite fairly enthusiastic though obviously embarrassed reviews, was ignored by the public, it was doubtless because the avowed intention of the film was to construct narrative structures—in images and sounds—based on the generalized division of any sign into its inverse, as with the "characters," the main actor: Boris/Robin. So we're dealing with a story that's essentially elusive.

Now it is actually the film's internal structure that's the arena for all the conflicts previously described. Each element of the story—each set, scene, bit of dialogue, object—is as if undermined by an internal split and the suspicion that it can only reappear elsewhere "returned," in both senses of the word: returned and turned around. So the whole story can only unfold through the cancellation of each thing into its opposite. However, Boris Varissa follows the ritual path: he speaks, corrects himself, goes on speaking, he imagines, he invents himself; thanks to his discourse he gradually insinuates himself into the hostile world of the castle, invades the girls' beds one after the other, grapples with the memory of the vanished Resistance fighter, tries to appropriate for himself the veneration of which that other is the object, and of course ends up killing the father, believing he will be master in his place, for good. But he's reckoned without his own double, his shadow, that other with whom he wanted to change places, the so-called comrade-in-arms, the *real* hero, "real" since his name is carved on the monument to the Resistance dead: Jean Robin. Boris is driven out like a pariah or a phantom, toward the forest from which he emerged right at the beginning (the *Urwald*?), whereas Jean returns without a word, secure as justice itself. And it's Jean, the good son returned from the dead, the one who lost his liberty to the law, who will replace the dead father and reign over the gynaeceum that's been set to rights.

We are told that the traditional conflict that relentlessly pits the always wicked father against the inevitably wicked son—right from his earliest childhood—is the origin of all subsequent rebellion against the law. Yet I have already stated that I've never felt a murderous impulse toward or even any sort of rivalry with the man who begot me, who nourished me, whose name I bear. Never *consciously*, the guardians of the psychoanalytical order will unhesitatingly reply. "Consciously" be damned! I've even consciously felt quite the opposite. Of course our doctors have rejected this disclaimer in advance. But the refusal to accept any disclaimer is the principal defect of all closed systems, which don't tolerate gaps, deviation, or disagreement.

I believe I chose the career of biologist and agronomist myself. Still, as I wasn't a child much given to questioning, my father could very well have chosen for me, without my knowing, since the family got along so well together. Anyway, that certainly wasn't the case with my career as a writer. When I made the sudden, scarcely justifiable decision to leave the Institut National de la Statistique et des Études Économiques (where for three years, along with six other engineers from the top schools, I contributed to the editing and reputation of the journal founded by Alfred Sauvy, *Etudes et conjoncture*) and launch into a novel (*Un Régicide*) that I hadn't written a word of, I might normally have incurred various paternal reproaches. Nothing of the sort happened: the abrupt interruption of a promising career met with no obstacles or remonstrances from my parents, and I was still living in the very modest family home. And although this first novel was rejected by Gallimard (a judgment that was a kind of litmus test at the time), when I repeated my offense a few years later, leaving the Institut des Fruits et Agrumes Coloniaux to devote myself entirely to writing *Les Gommes*, again everything went smoothly: my parents left me free, without the slightest reservation or expression of displeasure.

And yet they would have had the right to regret, if only *sotto voce*, the long and costly scientific studies they had allowed me to complete. There was never any question of it. On the contrary, Papa made every possible effort to smooth my way, negotiating with the landlord so that I could have a cheap, tiny garret of my own on Rue Gassendi; it was too cramped even for a small table, but I wrote three successive novels on my lap in this attic solitude, and lived there until my marriage in October 1957. Papa also offered to go on feeding me, three floors below, in return for a nominal sum.

And yet in his eyes writing offered no reasonable hope of social success, nor even the life of a recluse rewarded by fame; still less did he think of it as a possible way of earning a living. Things were a bit different with my mother, who in her youth had been attracted to belles lettres and had tried her hand at stories and poetry. Not so my father. My decision probably worried him, but since literature was my choice, albeit a late one, he soon found his own justification—and despite everything, pleasure—in doing all he could to enable me to devote myself to it freely.

An almost plausible explanation comes to mind: he was a *good* father because he was *mad*. Maman had always quite seriously maintained that Papa was slightly deranged, even suffering from recognizable mental disorders. She used to say that if I was intelligent, it came from her side, but if I was a genius (and of course she thought I was), it could only come from Papa, whose insanity, in my case, had luckily taken this fortunate turn. For the same reasons she always advised me not to have children (I followed her advice, not being particularly interested in babies, nor in little boys; as for little girls . . .). She thought that my father's abnormal nervous condition was the result of being a child of older parents, and that he'd passed his impaired chromosomes on to me. Her reading of *Le Voyeur* soon reinforced her fears for my psychic and sexual health. It was a fine book, she told me when I'd given her the manuscript, but "I would have preferred that it had not been written by my son." In a word, she was delighted that in my case potential infirmity had been transmuted into creativity, but it was best to stop there: in her opinion there was a very strong likelihood that the next generation would produce monstrosities rather than eccentricities. Maman would say all this with the same serene confidence she brought to all her decided, unconventional opinions.

She had a deep, solemn voice all the more persuasive in that she often spoke passionately. Then her tone was utterly positive: the unanswerable resolve of one who knows. And she must have "known" things, partly through her *reason*, but also perhaps through her very Breton sensitivity to *omens*. For example, several decades in advance she announced the precise date of her death, which was engraved with her initials—by an unknown hand—on the wooden base of the sewing

machine she bought secondhand from American surplus just after her marriage. And now sometimes, at
irregular intervals, I hear her voice again. It's usually in
the evening, before I go to bed or fall asleep, but it can
happen suddenly at any time of day. It usually lasts
about ten seconds. The sentences are clear, very vivid,
very near, and perfectly articulated. And yet I don't
know what she's saying. I only hear her tone of voice,
the resonance, the inflections—the song, as it were.

An image from the twenties, in Kerangoff, in the blazing
midsummer sun. . . . Is it a story I was told a long time
later? Anyway, I can see the scene as clearly as if I'd
been there. But how old was I? My father, on vacation,
is stretched out on his back on a small path through the
kitchen garden, just under a hedge of gooseberry
bushes, and is trying to catch the ripe fruit in his mouth
off the end of laden, flexible branches that droop almost
to the ground. From time to time he gives up and begins
to bellow like a wounded beast. Is it because of the long
thorns that make his task impossible, or is it only a
sudden fit of despair? Grandmother Canu, scandalized,
asks her daughter to put a stop to this incongruous din,
which will disturb the neighbors and ruin our reputation for miles around. My mother, not taking the thing
to heart, answers that with a husband like this she might
as well get used to some eccentricity or strange behavior. And she adds, "I'd like to see you in my shoes!"
"My poor daughter," protests Grandmother with dignity, "you wouldn't catch me making a mistake like
that!"

But at times we actually did witness more worrisome
crises, although they were short-lived. At the front Papa
was a sapper and had specialized in what was called the
"war of mines," which must have been particularly
appalling; he was still haunted by the memory ten years

later. They dug underground tunnels, crudely shored up, through the no-man's-land beyond the front lines; then, crawling along even narrower tunnels six or seven meters underground, they laid mines under the enemy trenches. But the enemy was digging under our tunnels too, and so on, deeper and deeper all the time, so that they never knew which of them would blow the other up first. Papa sometimes talked a little about the life of these men who were buried alive, and about the muffled thuds of the German pickaxes throbbing in the soil as if coming from all sides at once, getting faster, stopping suddenly, starting up again, louder now, breaking rhythm like a heart about to burst with anxiety, and yet—it was a matter of life and death—you had to estimate direction and distance accurately in order to alter your own course. Sergeant Major Robbe-Grillet had been hit several times, hence his multiple injuries . . .

In my early childhood Papa would quite often wake up in the middle of the night, having a nightmare. He'd rise up like a ghost, his cotton nightshirt floating around him, leap from the rumpled sheets, and run wild-eyed through the small apartment yelling "Put out the *calbombes*!" Maman, still in her armchair at the dining-room table, would calmly put down her paper and lead Papa back to bed, and soon to sleep, talking soothingly as if to a delirious child (*"Siehst du, Vater, den Erlkönig nicht?"*); then she would turn to her frightened children and reassure them as best she could. *Calbombes* must have been the miner's lamps that had to be put out quickly before an imminent explosion, I don't know why. . . . Or was it the opposite? Maybe he was shouting "Light the *calbombes*!" I don't remember anymore.

My father himself readily admitted that he wasn't really normal. It didn't bother him in the least. He would say with a half-smile, "I've got a screw loose . . ." Not, he explained, because his parents were elderly when he was born, but because of the war and his head injuries. For many years he'd been pleading his case at the appropriate ministries, and had been referred for expert opinions, in order to get himself officially declared "insane." To supplement his meager pension as an ex-serviceman with head wounds, decorations, etc., he was loud in his demands for additional, much more substantial compensation for permanent insanity resulting from cranial trauma suffered at the front: the shock of the explosions, shells bursting, etc. However, the experts weren't convinced, and the magistrates always dismissed his claim: maybe he was unhinged, but the war could not be held responsible!

My father's loose screw reminds me of another expression current in the family, referring to a particular kind of anguish or profound mental unease: "My head's full of streaks"; "This business gives me streaks in the head." The expression came from one of Kipling's stories, "The Disturber of Traffic," in which a lighthouse keeper goes mad in his lighthouse, lost in the treacherous waters between the Sunda Islands. He constantly sees streaks streaming over the surface of the sea below him, streaks of spindrift forming among the eddies and stretching out endlessly in parallel lines drifting with the current. He blames this unbearable phenomenon on the ships that use the straits, accusing them of "streaking" his personal territory, the floor of his dwelling, and even the inside of his brain. He reacts by sending out false signals to divert the traffic into other passages and so stop the ships from continuing to disturb the treacherous channel he watches over and with which he identifies . . .

In my childhood I spent hours watching little streaks of whitish spindrift tracing more or less regular patterns of parallel curves on the deceptively calm flowing water, everything sliding almost imperceptibly but continuously, always in the same direction, between the rocks at Brignogan, on that coast of granite and storms where my grandmother's father, whom I never knew, had been a sergeant in the coast guard. The family called him Grandfather Perrier. When we were very small, my sister and I were taken there from time to time—on the miniature railway from Brest, which seemed like a toy—to spend a few days in an old-fashioned stone cottage with very thick walls and narrow windows, very Spartan, built along the parapet walk by the shore, and only separated from it by a patch of garden washed at high tide by sea spray. It was "Perrine's house," unless I'm getting muddled—an old friend of the sergeant's two children, Grandmother Canu and Godmother, who had spent their entire youth in the village with the little peasant girls and fishermen's daughters, speaking mainly Breton, going in the evenings to one or another's house to read about the lives of the saints and listen to traditional tales of shipwrecks, ghosts, and wandering souls that they could hear keening in the starless night as they went back home in their clogs along sandy paths sodden with rain, where unleashed hordes of phantoms brushed against them, mingling with the gusts of the west wind.

Little streaks of whitish spindrift, sea swirling insidiously among huge heaps of pink granite blocks, sand hollowed out at the foot of the rocks by never-ending, almost invisible eddies, treacherous beaches and little waves whose regular motion was deceptively reassuring—this whole aquatic universe, as seductive as it was dangerous, gave me bad dreams. It reappears in several of my *Instantanés* and also in the nocturnal distress at the beginning of *Un Régicide*. But that novel and one of Kipling's longer stories have similarities that I only noticed recently, though they can't be coincidental. It's called "The Finest Story in the World." A young office clerk is troubled by persistent recurring visions, particularly clear and vivid ones that seem to belong to a previous life several hundred years ago, or maybe one or two thousand, when he was a galley slave. The harsh orders of the slave master, the cracking of the whip, the rhythmic movement of the oars, the nostalgic songs of his fellow oarsmen, and above all the huge wave that hangs suspended, towering over the gunwale just before the shipwreck, poised to break over the men chained to their benches. . . . All these images keep bursting in on him, more and more tangible and dramatic, until the day of his marriage when everything stops abruptly, leaving no trace. . . . Sisyphus, Kafka says, was a bachelor.

Grandfather Perrier, Marcelin Benoît Marie, doubtless had the job of watching over a small sector of the coastal zone, but what for? Was there possibly a bit of smuggling—tobacco, alcohol, fabric, contraband from England? I have heard talk of wreckers who lit gorse fires on the cliffs to mislead foreign ships and lure them onto the reefs, where they would break up, leaving scattered cargo and the debris of their shattered hulls to be pillaged. Yet most of these stories seem to belong to earlier times or to be the stuff of legends. On the other hand, real shipwrecks were common in those waters in bad weather, and the coast guard had to allocate the wreckage that washed ashore. And so, at Kerangoff, there was a bedroom in solid mahogany that came from Marcelin Perrier, made for the wedding of his daughter Mathilde (my grandmother) with billets of rare wood that had been deposited on the shores of his territory.

All the men of the family spent some time in the navy and were then coastguards till they retired. In the attic (it was Grandfather Perrier who had had our large wattle-and-daub house built) I found the service records of the last three generations, written in the spring of 1862 by François Perrier, my great-great-grandfather. Because I've always been moved by the laconic quality of that yellowed sheet of paper, I copy it out here as is, only adding punctuation. I think the text (rather than the paper itself, which seems to have been copied out later by another hand) was written by François, Marcelin's father, because it contains more details about him, especially about "*our* departure from Brest"—the first person must have slipped out despite his obvious concern to be objective.

"Perrier, Benoît, called Va-de-bon-coeur. Aquitaine regiment, seventeen years. 1778 war. Four years in India under Bailly de Suffren. Discharged at Vannes, barracks regimental depot, 1784. Coast guard service, twenty-six years. Died 20 November 1832.

"Perrier, François Jean Marie, younger son of Benoît. Five years six months service to the State, army and navy. Began service on a gunboat of the 21st convoy in the Channel, Captain Bozec, 11 January 1811. Discharged in May of the same year. Drafted to Brest for training until 17 August the same year, the day of our departure from Brest with a cadre of the 17th naval battalion, Captain Prateau. Left Boulogne with this battalion 22 March 1812, for Danzig in Prussia, and then for the Russian campaign. Transferred to the bridge train March 1813 at Mainz, after the retreat from Russia, and fought on in the 1813 campaign in Saxony and Silesia. Taken prisoner in the aftermath of Leipzig, under the walls of Targau in Bavaria, and taken to Berlin in Prussia in October the same year. Escaped from prison in November and returned to France 13 December the same year, to the fortress of Kehl. Sent to Brest with a travel warrant issued by the Strasbourg naval office, and arrived 24 December the same year. Attached to 16th naval battalion at Brest, Captain Bijoux, from 14 January 1814 to October the same year. Recalled in March 1815 for the Vendée campaign, in an emergency artillery company, Captain Conseille. Mustered out in October 1815. Coast guard service, twenty-seven years three months. Sainte-Hélène medal.

"Marcelin, Benoît Marie Perrier, older son of François Jean Marie. Five years five months in the navy on board the steam frigate *Asmodée*. Mustered out 15 May 1849 as quartermaster first class. Coast guard service, fifteen years as of the present (15 April 1862)."

Marcelin had married Marie-Yvonne Magueur, whose brother died in action at Toulon, and whose father was in charge of the postal service in Finistère. For him, as for all these sailors, soldiers, or coastguards, serving the State was a sort of sacred mission as well as an honor. One day he drove his carriage through a procession that to his mind was moving too slowly. Cutting off a procession! In those first years of the nineteenth century, in Brittany! To the outraged man of God who was brandishing his cross to ward off evil and prevent sacrilege, my ancestor Magueur, so they say, shouted majestically from his seat on high, "God in heaven, Father! The Mail must get through!" My family always liked to recount this act of civic courage in the face of clerical obscurantism and superstition.

Henri de Corinthe on his white horse, head high, sitting erect as usual, refusing to slump in the saddle but clearly swaying to the left, a position he often adopts after a long, tiring ride—Henri de Corinthe, on a calm night under a full moon, crosses the heather-clad country bordering a deserted cove on the jagged coastline of Léon. Just as the track he's following joins the narrow coastguard path beside the shore, his ear, attuned to the sounds of the sea, picks up a louder noise coming from the direction of the water, mingling with the regular splash of the ebb-tide waves, also rhythmic, yet sharper, stronger, more distinct.

Tightening the reins very slightly, he stops his horse to listen more carefully. It's like the repeated slapping of a vigorous paddle on wet washing: *floc-floc*. There is indeed a stream flowing into the beach at this spot, but who'd be washing by moonlight away from all human habitation? Corinthe immediately thinks of the old peasant belief in "nocturnal washerwomen": young women from the spirit world, harbingers of ill fortune, rather like the witches in *Macbeth*. Smiling to himself, he wonders if they're about to announce his imminent accession to the throne of Scotland. (The Corinthe family has distant ancestors in Wales and Northumberland, among them the famous Lord Corynth who fought against Cromwell.) Comte Henri approaches the tiny fault hollowed out by the running water and follows it to the beach.

Just before he gets there, the streambed widens out to form a sort of small pool. It would, in a pinch, be a possible spot for washing, and lying sideways at the edge of the shimmering pool there actually is one of those rough wooden boxes where country women kneel to beat their washing with a paddle. But the worn device seems to be abandoned, and there's no one in sight. Besides, although the sound is more and more distinct, it seems to be coming from farther away, as if from the sea itself. Well, the intrepid rider remarks inwardly, this nocturnal washerwoman doesn't seem to mind washing in salt water! And more intrigued than ever, he spurs his horse across the strip of sand to the water's edge.

There's not a living soul here either, not in front of him nor to the right nor to the left, down the whole length of the sweeping curve festooned with white spindrift sparkling in the pale nocturnal light. The ground's fairly hard in this part of the bay, so the horse's hooves aren't likely to sink in. Corinthe urges his beast toward the open sea, into the shallows that just come up to its knees. The odd slapping sound is now very close, and soon, about twenty meters away, the man sees a flat object dancing on the crest of the waves, rising with each, then dropping back into the trough of the next, and gleaming with an extraordinary light.

After a few more steps—more difficult because the horse is resisting—Corinthe realizes it's a mirror, kept afloat by its thick oval frame, the upturned glass reflecting the moon's rays at the rider depending on the angle. But when he wants to cross the few meters that still separate him from the piece of wreckage, his faithful horse refuses to move. At first Corinthe thinks it's because of the waves, which are now a bit rougher and at times come up to the horse's chest. So he waits a few seconds for his mount to adjust before spurring him gently forward.

Then the animal rears up terrified and begins to jerk his neck violently, obviously trying to turn around, at the same time opening his mouth wide to get rid of the bit. The rider tries to master this unusual, incomprehensible resistance. He's stimulated by the battle and all the more agitated as the coveted object is now moving away, doubtless towed by the ebbing tide. And still the mocking *floc-floc* goes on, even more vigorously, beating a more aggressive rhythm, more vehement each time the oval mirror—which must be very heavy—drops back into the liquid expanse.

Although there's hardly any wind, the waves suddenly seem much bigger and rougher than is usual at low tide in this fairly sheltered cove. The horse is now maddened, his master can't hold him. When an even larger wave breaks over them, the beast rears up vertically and succeeds in unhorsing Comte Henri. Managing to regain his footing in the icy water, he watches in despair as his mount, nostrils flaring, turns around instantly and gallops toward dry land, neighing continuously, head straining backward like a wolf baying at the moon. Spindrift rises beneath his hooves, and the spray mingles with his sparkling white windswept mane in a bluish light that suddenly flares up with the radiance of an apocalyptic vision.

However, Corinthe struggles fiercely, although unhorsed, now swimming despite his heavy, waterlogged clothes, now wading when he regains his footing in the interval between two waves, then jerked out of his depth again, pulled under the heavy seas, losing his balance and his breath for seconds at a time, stunned, tossed about, dragged farther and farther out by the receding piece of wreckage. But in a last burst of energy he gains enough ground—God knows how—to grasp it. The object seems so heavy that Corinthe wonders by what miracle it's staying afloat. The exhausted man is afraid he'll never manage to bring it ashore, he feels as if he's carrying a dead weight. The oval frame is more than a meter high, and the carved wood is as solid as a ship's gunwale. Corinthe hangs on with all his strength. He battles desperately against the tide, which seems to be pulling in the opposite direction, and he has no idea how long his struggle goes on . . .

Thanks to a superhuman effort, he at last succeeds in accomplishing the absurd task he felt compelled to take on. He drags his prize out of the water, utterly exhausted, and drops to the sand as if to fall asleep on the spot. But he's trembling with cold, weariness, and nerves. His muscles contract in a series of involuntary, painful spasms. And his mind's gone blank.

When he opens his eyes again, he sees his white horse leaning over him, looking down at him with a very human expression of sadness, or anxiety, or reproach. Comte Henri turns away, half raising himself on an elbow, and looks at the mirror lying beside him among scraps of seaweed and shells left by the ebbing tide. The huge carved frame seems to be made of jacaranda or some dark mahogany from South America. The glass itself is tarnished, doubtless from prolonged immersion in the sea; the surface is sprinkled with drops of water that are beginning to dry. But in the cloudy depths of the

71

thick glass, its glaucous tints accentuated by the wan moonlight, Henri de Corinthe distinctly sees—and almost without surprise—the reflection of the gentle, fair face of his lost fiancée, Marie-Ange, who drowned off a beach in the Atlantic near Montevideo, and whose body was never found. She is there in the mirror, her pale blue eyes staring at him, a mysterious smile on her face.

A short while later—a few minutes at most—Corinthe must have lost consciousness. A coastguard from Brignogan on his morning rounds was astonished to find a solitary, magnificent white horse in the middle of the beach, a rich man's horse with a fine black leather saddle and nickel stirrups that sparkled despite the overcast sky, but with the bridle hanging from its neck. He approached and immediately discovered the body lying in the sand beside a large oval mirror in a carved mahogany frame, such a deep red that at times it seemed like ebony.

Lying on his back, the man looked like a corpse. The rising waters—it was almost high tide at that hour—were lapping the rider's boots. But his clothes, which must certainly have been very elegant a few hours before, were so thoroughly soaked that the coastguard's first thought was that he had a drowned man on his hands, washed ashore by the sea. And yet the proximity of the horse, which could hardly have been shipwrecked on a pleasure cruise with his master (whose clothes perfectly matched the luxurious trappings of the animal), made this hypothesis unlikely.

On the off chance, the conscientious officer decided to take the usual measures to expel water from the lungs, in case this really was a drowning and there might still be time. The only result after a few moments' effort was that the corpse opened its eyes and revealed itself to be very much alive, but so disturbed by goodness knows what adventure that the man still hadn't budged and was equally incapable of uttering a word. He didn't even seem to understand the pressing questions of the uniformed personage who had just erupted into his dream, and whom he stared at wild-eyed as if desperately trying to come down to earth.

After making sure that there was nothing broken in that solid, well-built body, the coastguard, who was uncommonly strong despite his small stature, succeeded without too much difficulty in getting the rider to his feet. But there was no question of hoisting him onto his horse in his present state. So the best solution seemed to be to help the invalid to a small bar at the end of the next cove (at Ker-an-Dû, where a narrow tarmac track led to some fishermen's cottages) and wait for a doctor, while the horse could carry the mirror, which the officer was sure belonged to the stranger.

But when he cautiously made to put the heavy, fragile object on the saddle, intending to fasten it with the reins as best he could, the beast, as if suddenly panic-stricken (until then it had been standing very quietly, if a little distance away), reared up on its hind legs whinnying, then dropped down heavily and began to back away snorting violently, its four legs splayed, head lowered in such an extraordinary attitude that the coastguard himself took fright.

The mirror was too heavy for him to carry up to the inn, so he decided to leave it there, merely putting it at the top of the beach out of reach of the high tide so he could have it fetched later by some seaweed gatherer's cart. Then he returned to Corinthe, who had watched the whole scene without saying a word, impassive, still standing on the spot where he'd been left, but swaying on his stiff legs and obviously in no state to take a step on his own.

While he was doing his best to support a considerable part of the weight of this tall, weak body leaning against his chest as they went on their hazardous way, tottering along the narrow, awkward path, the coastguard reflected on the mirror's inexplicable presence on the beach. In fact it wasn't very likely that this elegant horseman—however strong he might be—had been riding with such a heavy, cumbersome burden. Then maybe it was just a piece of wreckage thrown up on the coast; and in that case it would belong to the State and not to the stranger who'd found it. Unless he'd swum into the sea and fished it out, which hardly seemed compatible with his outfit: why would he have worn clothing so unsuitable for such a dangerous undertaking? And anyway, even if this were the case, wasn't he himself within his rights to claim a third of the prize? All the same, the claim would only be satisfied provided no other heir or owner showed up within the time prescribed by law.

There remained, however, an even more disquieting possibility: that those three elements—horse, mirror, and rider—had converged on that shore by pure chance, with no link between them at all, neither of causality nor of ownership. While the two intertwined men stagger on their hazardous path across the countryside, the pensive horse three meters behind, the excessively scrupulous guardian of public order progressively loses himself in the combined complications of maritime law and problematic hypotheses . . .

From this point on, what happened next is much more obscure. It certainly does seem that Henri de Corinthe reached the hamlet in much better shape. Maybe the painful walk on the arm of his savior had helped to revive him? Doubtless he didn't want to wait for the unpredictable arrival of a doctor, the alcohol-laced coffee that the innkeeper normally served the seamen having sufficed to relieve his dazed condition. But it is also said that he had to be put to bed as soon as he arrived at the inn and was wracked by such a high fever that for several days there were even fears for his sanity.

In his delirium he murmured partially inaudible, incoherent, disjointed sentences in which a dead young woman was constantly mentioned; at moments it seemed that he had accidentally killed her himself, at others that she had disappeared, shipwrecked on a boat equipped for deep-sea diving. One of the peculiarities of his story, which made it almost impossible to follow— apart from its excessive fragmentation, contradictions, gaps, and repetitions—was that he kept switching from the past to the present tense though he seemed to be going over the same period of his life and the same events.

However, one thing is certain: the very day he made his dramatic entrance into the cramped, dark bar at Keran-Dû, where a small group of fishermen at the tables suddenly fell silent, turning their heads one after the other toward the open door through which he had just entered (in the firm grip of his uniformed keeper)—that very day, mysteriously eluding all surveillance, Corinthe supposedly returned on horseback to the scene of his nocturnal adventure, evidently intent on retrieving his formidable treasure. To reconcile the two apparently incompatible versions—his rapid recovery or his prolonged stay in bed—one can imagine that the sick man, mastering his fever and misleading his obviously anxious hosts about the real state of his health, actually slipped away very soon with some excuse or other, and thanks to the reflexes of a seasoned horseman, managed to ride to that maleficent beach (or so it was considered in a whole series of legends and local superstitions that I often heard in my childhood).

Although the final sequence of the episode (called "the ghost in the mirror") will forever remain extremely confused, since accounts vary considerably and are mixed up with vague memories of folklore, there are a certain number of indisputable points we can use as guidelines. When Corinthe comes in sight of the cove—which he has remembered clearly—and anxiously scans the curve from the top of the dune covered with pink heather and clumps of sea thrift, he realizes at once that the mirror has disappeared. The tide is going out, and a wide, silky strip of sand sloping in an inviting hollow is already exposed, forming a new, perfectly smooth golden stretch where the morning's ebb for once hasn't left any seaweed or other debris, so that the smallest bit of wreckage would be visible at a glance.

Nor is there any trace of what the horseman seeks on the dry, ridged sand at the foot of the dune where the high tide didn't reach. The bay is as calm as a lake, ruling out the possibility of a recent storm during which the raging sea could have swept away various objects left on the coast. On the contrary, the whole atmosphere is so peaceful that Corinthe, as if forgetting a bad dream, is moving along at an easy gait on his white horse, itself quite soothed now, when suddenly, reaching the channel carved out by the stream in the sloping shoreline, he again catches sight of the laundry box, left beside the translucent pool by a nocturnal washerwoman.

The wooden device isn't in such a bad state as he'd thought in the deceptive moonlight. It's only that the oak is bleached and worn from use. You would swear that someone has just this minute been using it. Three steps more and Corinthe discovers (and it's almost as if he'd come to this spot unconsciously seeking just this, so strong is his feeling that he was expecting it), hanging from the higher heather that covers the other side of the hollow where the little stream flows, three articles of freshly washed feminine lingerie drying in a sudden ray of sunshine—a thin, improbable beam of yellow light slanting down out of the gray sky.

Because of the delicate refinement of the silk, with its enchanting old-fashioned embroidery, these couldn't possibly be the underclothes of a simple peasant girl. Aren't they actually . . . Have mercy! My God, have

mercy! The torn chemisette, the tiny triangle, the lace—
here the man on the white horse remembers having
once . . . Have mercy! Have mercy! On the slender, lacy
panties and matching garter belt there are large, fresh
bloodstains that seem to be seeping through—scarlet
stains shining unbearably bright.

Henri de Corinthe would then have felt a great chill
creeping rapidly through his limbs, his chest, his whole
body. And there's nothing strange in that if we consider
that—apparently—he hadn't even changed his clothes
since his prolonged immersion the night before. Doubtless it was this terrible chill that brought on a serious
pulmonary ailment, which also provides a perfectly rational explanation for the enforced stay at the inn, the
high fever, and the delirium.

But it's also said that from then on, the faithful horse
with its blond mane was strange, skittish, difficult. Brignogan folk say that horses can't see their reflections and
that in the glaucous depths of the foundering mirror,
instead of the face of Marie-Ange, the murdered fiancée
who was pursuing his master, the white horse for the
first time saw his own image, which is to say, his death.
The firm belief that that night the animal changed into a
sort of demon or specter was strengthened in the eyes of
the credulous peasants by the fact (which was moreover
confirmed) that the sound of his hooves was never
heard, even when he was galloping over hard ground.

Even today no one doubts that the horse was bewitched, if only because of its lively grace and exceptional beauty, and yet even the rough date of this
incident of the mirror remains a mystery. In principle
the scene ought to have taken place quite a long time
before the defeat of 1940, as many details that I remember attest: the wild aspect of the North Finistère coast,
which has since been so badly despoiled, the coast-

guard's traditional daily round along the cliff, and even his uniform, the dark old bar at Ker-an-Dû, etc.

Then too, we mustn't forget that the injury Corinthe sustained at the front definitely prevented him from riding. Everyone remembers his stiff leg and silver-topped cane, which not only helped his balance and made his limp less noticeable but also gave him a dandy's gait that he turned to his advantage, enhancing his elegance and prestige. Now, Marie-Ange van de Reeves, the dead young mistress whose charming yet reproachful face unexpectedly reappeared in the phantom mirror, died while visiting Uruguay with Henri de Corinthe, who—we know for certain—did not live in South America until after the end of the war. Had he had some love affair there before? It's unlikely. Didn't his intense political activity in the thirties, given his clientele, preclude any shady honeymoons, crime or accident aside, even on the other side of the Atlantic, by the distant shores of La Plata?

But I sometimes think I'm confusing the fair Marie-Ange with another pretty girl, Angélica von Salomon, who was also very close to the young count. And perhaps I'm unconsciously giving Corinthe character traits, military feats, or more anodyne biographical details that don't belong to him but are borrowed from other more or less famous personalities of the time: Henri de Kerillis, François de La Rocque, or even the Comte de Paris, who was also called Henri and was a pretender to the throne of France.

Like many ex-servicemen disillusioned by the victory that had cost them so dearly, anxious patriots increasingly disenchanted with the parliamentary regime, my father belonged to the Croix de Feu at the beginning of the thirties. But its founder, Colonel de La Rocque, was subsequently suspected of using his troops on February 6, 1934, to protect the Palais-Bourbon in secret collusion with Daladier's police. The accusation, which I think came from Action Française, of course can't be verified, but it illustrates perfectly the multiple divisions and sectarian quarrels that existed among the extreme right-wing factions.

Besides, it was only in 1936, or even at the beginning of the following year, that Corinthe, disregarding the advice of his closest friends, officially founded his own group: the *Renaissance Socialiste Nationale* (though in his youth he had been elected deputy on a monarchist ticket thanks to a short-lived experiment with full proportional representation). The movement had little success and was almost instantly forgotten; there were too many small parties with very similar aims arguing over the somewhat limited possibilities for militant action, and often quite reticent in the face of the declamatory, aggressive, and vacuous character of the platforms. Today it is more with boredom than regret, yet with some surprise, that I rediscover these more or less profascist civic passions, this disillusionment, even bitterness, echoed in the "character" of Laura throughout my first novel, *Un Régicide*.

Corinthe's different political hats (didn't he also have a brief flirtation with the Communist party during one of the most Stalinist periods in its history?) were probably just ways of expressing his own uncertainty and increasing anguish in the face of mounting danger. To die with panache in a futile battle against the armored divisions of the enemy—which was precisely, through an ironic twist of fate, that Germany whose spectacular recovery (and to a degree at least, ideology) he admired—was certainly a solution he had contemplated with equanimity. He had returned with a limp, albeit as elegant as ever, ready to throw himself wholeheartedly into the most dubious causes.

In his memoirs as director of the Théâtre-Français, David Samuelson says that just after his adolescence

Corinthe dreamed of becoming a great actor and that
he'd performed in small Parisian theaters, sometimes
even playing major roles. He showed a marked prefer-
ence for historical dramas in which he played solitary
heros with imposing, gloomy destinies: Napoleon, Ber-
lioz, Cromwell. . . . In this context Samuelson notes that
every politician is a failed actor. The opposite could just
as well be maintained.

Toward the end of the thirties the financial situation in
my father's cardboard box factory gradually improved.
In addition to the summer vacation, which we always
spent in Kerangoff at our maternal grandmother's (we
also went to the sea for shorter periods, staying in a
peasant's cottage near Quiberon that my mother's elder
sister had renovated), we began to take short winter
holidays too, in the Juras, this time with real skis and all
the necessary equipment, which we would lovingly get
ready weeks in advance. (Those were the days of
greased boots, bindings with adjustable straps, and Nor-
wegian tar wax, whose strong resin smell permeated the
apartment.)

Since Grandfather Robbe's death we no longer went
to Arbois, where we'd enjoyed the sensuousness of autumn with him, gathering the windfalls and fresh nuts
along the paths as the countryside turned to russet. (An
enlarged, slightly blurred sepia-tinted photograph with
the château in the background surrounded by leafless
trees shows me at seven or eight in a cotton smock that
looked like a little dress, encircling the flowering holly-
hocks with my bare arm, my curly brown head tilted
toward them as I smile winningly at the camera, graceful as a girl.)

But my father's brother—quite a bit older than he—
was postmaster at Le Russey, near Morteau, in the
Doubs. It was there that we learned to glide over gentle

but not very snowy slopes, in clearings between the firs. We stayed at a small café-hotel for traveling salesmen that my uncle used to frequent. He was a debonair man, often a bit drunk, a Sunday painter in oils: winter landscapes—cottages and forests in the snow—not from life, since he didn't like to leave town, but copied from postcards. His work was for sale, exhibited among the crates of fruit and vegetables at the neighborhood grocer's. The firs in his pictures looked like herring bones, as he cheerfully agreed. Then, joking and punning, he would dwell on his frustrations as a misunderstood artist.

The scenes that stick in our memory most clearly are usually the most insignificant, pointless ones: they stay in our heads forever, but we don't know what to do with them. Here's one that for no reason at all insists on being included in my story. I went back to visit this Uncle Maurice ten years later. He had retired to Ornans, and since I remembered him as a likable man, I decided to drop in unannounced while I was on a cycling trip from the Vosges to the Alps with Claude Ollier, whom I'd just met in the labor camp in Germany.

I had a great deal of trouble finding where the ex-postmaster lived because he was calling himself Robbe, having dropped half of his too complicated name, which had nevertheless been in the family for at least ten generations. The place wasn't exactly a hovel, but almost, as I thought at the time and still do today—gloomy, dingy, and dilapidated. I have to climb a rough wooden staircase with several steps missing or loose, and just at the top there's a hole in the floor barely concealed by a bit of roofing felt. My uncle and aunt have been drinking as usual. The liter of red wine is there on the table among a pile of utensils that are difficult to identify. The whole room is so cluttered with miscellaneous objects that I don't know where to put myself. At last Uncle Maurice recognizes me, or anyway realizes I'm his brother's son. Aunt Louise, in a drunken

81

stupor, is collapsed in a corner on such a low chair that at first I thought she was sitting on the floor, a fat, shapeless bundle with a puffy red face on top. Every thirty seconds she repeats in the same peevish, scared voice, "Who's there, Maurice?"

They both died soon after. My father went to the funeral (at Ornans, O Courbet!) and brought back a couple of things to remember them by: a small cherry-wood sofa from Arbois with a curious folding back (it's now here at Le Mesnil) and two gold wedding rings found in a pin tray. I adopted them on my wedding day, never having known for whom they were made. The larger one only fit my right ring finger, but there was no church or priest to reproach me. So I've been wearing it on that finger for more than a quarter of a century now. It took the place of the four aluminum bands I mentioned earlier, which had worn thin and brittle. The narrower ring was made even smaller and repolished for Catherine. As for Aunt Louise's anxious question, I'm quite sure it was the *formant* for the phrase "Don't shoot, Maurice!" in *Les Gommes*, at the point where the police inspector is imagining a sordid version of Daniel Dupont's murder.

After two years we abandoned Le Russey for a tiny village in the Haut-Jura, which we visited regularly until the war; the mountains were much more pictur-esque, and the skiing conditions were better. There was always lots of snow, sometimes too much. We were enchanted. "Putting on your skis at the hotel door" seemed an undreamt-of happiness. There were no offi-cial ski slopes then, and you went up by tying sealskins under your skis, but there was a variety of suitable courses, and coming down was easy. All four of us were happy there—or more often, all three, since mother wasn't so strong—alone in the world in the white mountains that suddenly turn pink and blue at dusk, as we come back single file through stretches of virgin snow bordered by pine trees swaying under new fur coats that the night frost will freeze, thin black silhouettes slowly advancing along the shelf, apparently motionless from a distance, the father in his alpine huntsman's gear leading the way, followed by his two children one behind the other; happy, too, to see Maman again and tell her of our feats and find the warm lights of the comfortable little hotel, which was situated exactly on the border, with the front door in France and the back door in Switzerland, something that amused us immensely. (Our favorite rooms were the ones cut right down the middle by the theoretical line separating the two nations.) Winter sports hotels have a very special smell when you come back to them from the cold air outside; it's so unique that I won't even try to analyze it, but I've felt that thrill again, intact, many years later in Davos or Zermatt.

During that whole period my mother was often ill (and we always had to take this into account, for vacations and everything else); in fact she had a classic fibroma but refused to have an operation—out of respect for nature, she would explain—preferring to stay in bed for days on end reading her papers. My father was never in the least reluctant to do the daily shopping, washing up, or other domestic chores. Since we were relatively better off now, an invaluable, devoted housekeeper—a formidable Swiss woman whose speech was coarse and racy—took over the cleaning and cooking; she made vast apple tarts and kept the extremely thin puff pastry a state secret (she would shut herself off in the tiny kitchen to make it, and we could hear her loud exclamations accompanied by the sound of the rolling pin, wielded vigorously like a bat, as though to destroy everything in sight), and in fact she ruled as thoroughly as she scoured the little apartment on Rue Gassendi, where we now had a Moroccan carpet and frosted glass ceiling lights with brass trim, in that 1935 style that's coming back into fashion again.

This good lady stayed with us a long time—before, during, and after the war—but she always seemed to storm in like a whirlwind. When she arrived early each morning (we were still in bed sometimes), she would "adjust" the windows, meaning that she would fling them wide open on all sides, even in the dead of winter, so that the strongest possible drafts blew through the house. She then began to "clean the pigsty," that is, to do battle with untidiness. In the midst of the ensuing storm, with doors slamming and curtains flying, she first hid anything left lying around, often in the most unexpected places, saying that that would teach us to put our things away, and then she would sweep so energetically that the wooden broom hit the walls and furniture, which still bear the marks. Once we found her in the dining room standing on the sideboard: she'd decided to clean the top with the steel wool usually used on the oak floor, which also suffered in its less resilient parts.

When we got home at midday, there was no need to ask what she'd cooked for us, since she would invariably say that she'd made "noddels" (at least that's how I imagined the spelling) and when we'd ask what that was, she would answer with a loud, devastating laugh, "Prunes in shit!" Then, possibly hoping to make us share her enthusiasm, or merely to prolong the inexplicable joy her answer unfailingly gave her, she would immediately repeat it two or three times.

When war was declared, all the debts from the cardboard box factory had finally been paid, and my father decided to turn over his share in the business to his only brother-in-law and take various administrative jobs, first in the armaments ministry and then, after the armistice, in other similar kinds of organizations. A little later, thanks to the connections he'd maintained in the doll manufacturing world, he joined the Chambre Syndicale des Fabricants de Jouets, where he became secretary-general just about the time I began writing. He enjoyed acting the part of an official, sending himself up as he played at being the important gentleman attending professional meetings, traveling abroad, meeting government ministers; and he showed off a bit when he wore a new suit, as he had in the past, as the dashing Lieutenant Robbe-Grillet in his uniform at the Hagondange steelworks, where Yvonne Canu, our future mother, was a stenographer-typist.

My parents were obviously Pétainists, but unlike the usual kind, they were still Pétainists—maybe even more so—after the Liberation. Around 1955, I began to invite some of my new writer friends home, staunch leftists several of whom had been active in the Resistance. At the time my father had a passion for porridge: every evening for dinner he cooked up a batch of gray gruel— very tasty, as they say in Brittany—made with milk and slowly stirred with a wooden spoon, and he cheerfully served large helpings to all the visitors. Michel Zéraffa, Jean Duvignaud, or Lucien Goldmann would share his meal and conceal their surprise on seeing a large photo of Pétain in khaki smiling above the sideboard (the one where the steel wool had made a large dent to remove a tiny scratch), placed in the most prominent spot against the raffia wallpaper. They would politely avert their gaze, endeavoring not to see the shocking anachronism. But Duvignaud, the sophisticated man of the world, said one day between spoonfuls of porridge, as if it were merely an oversight, "Ah, so you've kept the Marshal's photo?" In fact that same photo had adorned nine out of ten French homes for four years. "No, not at all," my father answered, "I haven't kept it, I put it up on purpose the day the American troops entered Paris." And he had. Under the German occupation he hadn't seen any reason to advertise such conformist, officially sanctioned veneration on our walls, but he already felt an unreserved affection and respect for the legitimate head of state. For him Marshal Pétain was the soldier of 1914, he was the trenches, Verdun, the slow recovery of our armies at the time of our greatest despair, and finally he was victory. The signing of the armistice in 1940 was also credited to his wisdom and courage, whereas he had no part in the defeat. The historic handshake at Montoire demonstrated above all his integrity as a soldier. Curiously, this professional soldier was even credited with underlying antimilitarism for the sake of the family cause. And we weren't going to lose any sleep over the scrapping of political parties or over defunct parliamentary debates! Out of loyalty to Pétain, against the wicked rebellious son De Gaulle, my father even made a strict point of voting Communist for several years, having resolved to do so, he said, until the ashes of the old marshal were transferred to Douaumont to be placed beside his infantrymen.

My parents were confirmed anglophobes, a position that certainly seems to contradict what I've said about the English literature—for children or otherwise—that we'd been brought up on from our early childhood. But that was to a large extent under the influence of one of my mother's girlhood friends, a bookbinder in Paris who led a precarious existence, half bohemian, half poverty-stricken. This Henriette Olgiatti, whose grandfather Magnus claimed to be a direct descendant of Charlemagne (as she would tell us with her sarcastic yet warm laugh, which inevitably turned into an interminable coughing fit), was of Jewish origin and much drawn to British culture. With her brilliant, lively mind and wide culture, speaking a highly literary language easily and playfully, she probably played a considerable part in forming our tastes, particularly in the vast, indefinable realm of humor. She spent a great deal of time at our house under any pretext, smoked two packs of Camels a day, and bubbled over with anecdotes—if only about her own misfortunes—when she wasn't reading to us (*Just-So Stories, The Water Babies*, or *Captain Corcoran*). Papa often had to throw her out late at night so that everyone could finally get some sleep.

So for us hatred of England was strictly political, but it certainly didn't date from the last war. On the contrary, our common military reversals only served to rekindle ancient animosities: throughout my childhood I'd been lulled to sleep with old sea chanteys, from "Primauguet" to "Trente et un du mois d'août," that are hardly flattering to our neighbors across the Channel. And we were told with some emotion about the case of the fishermen forgotten on a little island at the tip of Brittany, who were rescued by policemen toward the end of the summer of 1914 and informed somewhat belatedly about the general mobilization; without a moment's hesitation regarding their hereditary enemy, they shouted, "This time we'll stuff their arrogance down their throats, the English swine!"—only to be thoroughly disappointed when they realized their mistake.

The course of the fighting in the North in 1940, the evacuation of Dunkirk ("After you, your lordships," people sneered), then the destruction of our defenseless fleet at Mers-el-Kébir, where hundreds of Breton sailors died (as the gravestones at the Recouvrance cemetery in the corner of our Kerangoff plain bear witness)— everything conspired to rekindle age-old feelings of distrust, ever ready to break out in violent execration of "Perfidious Albion," which returned the compliment.

87

At the least opportunity the same thing happens to-day: the French people quietly gloat when a French-built missile sinks a British warship off the islands we persist in calling the Malvinas, and if a referendum were held, our votes would speedily expel this treacherous ally from the Common Market, since she only appears to have joined in order to scuttle it more effectively. (I am writing these lines at the end of March 1984.)

So German propaganda was on very safe ground when it shamelessly exploited the rich vein of an-glophobia in the French, calling willy-nilly on Joan of Arc and Cato the Elder ("England, like Carthage . . ."), even republishing Willette's cruel sketches or insulting pamphlets dating from the Boer War, which my whole family, seething with rage, thoroughly enjoyed. The heroic resistance of our former partners during the Blitz counted for nothing in our eyes: as usual the English were defending their own interests, not ours. And if they energetically repulsed overt or insidious pressure from certain more or less germanophile American busi-ness interests, it was only because they couldn't bear to see their eternal nightmare realized: a European federa-tion. That the leader of the federation would be a mad-man called Hitler was merely a minor consideration in their eyes.

Maybe this was my parents' opinion too in a way, since their nationalism didn't prevent them from being confirmed supporters of a united, not to say unified, Europe (but without the English, heaven forbid!). So if they quoted with total conviction the saying attributed to a British statesman (Disraeli?)—"When I'm hesitat-ing between two solutions, I have only to decide which will do the most harm to France"—their position *vis-à-vis* a victorious Germany could only be ambivalent. Prussian militarism and thirst for conquest was a dan-ger, of course; but on the other hand, one day or an-other there must be one Europe, and it must include Germany (Nazi or not). The periodic wars on the Rhine or the Moselle made no sense, were merely the perpetuation of a tragic mistake. Let's forget these border disputes between two nations with the same interests at heart; they're as outdated as the medieval quarrels that once tore France apart . . .

Despite his rigid sense of honor, it wouldn't have taken much to persuade my father to find excuses for those (numerous?) soldiers of 1940 who didn't want to fight. The war against Germany reminded him too vividly of four nightmare years: mud, cold, shrapnel, poison gas, enemy trenches cleaned out with bayonets, men dying with their entrails hanging out, howling all night between the barbed wire—and all for nothing. Since we were unable to establish bonds of cooperation and friendship with Germany when we were the victors, we had to try now as the losers.

Such a gamble certainly went hand in hand with an unshaken confidence in the destiny of France, which, freed from the misguided rule of republican demagogy, would soon find her soul again and end up imposing her genius alongside the complementary genius of her first cousins. After all, we had already been conquered by Rome: two peoples often have a great deal to gain when they unite their conflicting qualities.

My father and mother firmly believed in the Franco-German partnership as the center of a larger future confederation, although as staunch supporters of Maurras they should have counted instead on our "Latin sister." At school they had made us learn German as our first foreign language, and we took no English at all since as gifted pupils we were studying Latin and Greek. Later, when my sister and I had to take another language for the exams, we chose Spanish.

However, after the defeat this "collaborationist" spirit was never translated into action, neither in the form of commitment to any party, nor in any personal fraternization with the occupying forces. The "silence of the sea" was the rule for us too, as a matter of dignity: a

hand held out to the conqueror was not to be confused
with an eagerness to lick his boots. But in a symbolic
gesture my father had buried the hatchet in a way:
when the Germans ordered civilians to surrender their
personal weapons, he went out—sick at heart, I
imagine—and threw the useless flare gun he'd brought
back from the front into the sewer.

My parents were anti-Semitic, and they freely admitted
it to anyone who cared to listen (even to our Jewish
friends, if they got the chance). I wouldn't wish to gloss
over such an awkward point. Anti-Semitism still exists
almost everywhere, in various more or less insidious
forms, and is always likely to break out again and wreak
havoc, like a fire left smoldering in a heap of embers
carelessly left untended. To fight successfully against
such a widespread, tenacious ideology it is first of all
essential not to make it a taboo subject.

It seems to me that my family's anti-Semitism was of
a fairly common type: neither militant (turning a Jew
over to German or Vichy persecution would naturally
have been abhorrent), nor religious (the god *they* had
crucified was obviously not ours), nor contemptuous
(as with the Russians), nor obsessive (as in Céline), nor
even involving antipathy (Jews could be exciting to read
or pleasant to know, like anyone else). Extremely irrational nevertheless, as in its more virulent forms, my
parents' anti-Semitism seems to have been specifically
"right-wing," since it was obviously motivated by a
basic concern for the maintenance of moral order, along
with a deep-seated distrust of all internationalism.

Just as Communists are always suspected of working
for the Soviet Union, which they are thought to cherish
as their true native land, so the Jews were at first accused of belonging to a very powerful supranational
community that was much more important to them

than their French passports. With no real "roots" in France, they were allegedly bound spiritually and by origin to a "land" other than ours; and they themselves would always feel more or less stateless. International capitalism was a related category, often incorporated in the term "Judeo-plutocrats," as if there weren't many more poor Jews in the world than millionaires, and as if all arms dealers were Israelites.

Even more disturbing is the notion of the Jews sowing the seeds of moral dissolution. For not only were the Hebrew people in exile considered alien to our national essence, they were also said to be immigrants of a particularly pernicious kind, spreading general uncertainty, the breakdown of conscience, domestic and political chaos from one end of old Europe to the other—in brief, swiftly bringing about the ruin of all organized society, the death of all healthy nations.

Today, using a vocabulary that certainly wasn't ours at the time, I would say that Jews throughout the world could be seen as unique fermenters of liberty. Of course this too is merely a stereotype; otherwise many Israeli generals and the majority of zealot rabbis would no longer be entitled to call themselves Jews. However, if we stick to this imagery, it's not just the morbid taste for misfortune, catastrophe, and despair, which is so readily attributed to them (while at the same time they're accused of amassing fortunes at the expense of the social body whose parasites they supposedly are), that reminds me precisely of what Heidegger says of anguish: the price to be paid for achieving freedom of mind at last.

It is here that the irreducible opposition between the notions of order and liberty appears quite clearly to me, crassly embodied in the two stereotyped portraits of the German people and the Jewish people. In particular, this explains the xenophobic sliding scale we used to exclude the Jews from the community, when they'd often been French for several generations, in order to attempt a union with the Germans, who were not French at all. But they at least were on the right side: the side of order.

To combat the formidable virus of contagious negation and metaphysical anguish (that is, of liberty), my parents were certainly far from imagining any "final solution." They were perfectly satisfied with the "reasonable" *numerus clausus* advocated by Maurras. Like many sincere people during the Occupation, we obviously didn't know that the Nazis were about to take quite different steps. Most of the Jews who were deported didn't know themselves. As for my mother, she always considered the organized mass extermination of the Jews so inconceivable that she continued to deny the reality of genocide right up to her death in 1975. She saw it as a simple matter of Zionist propaganda and faked documents: after all, people had also tried to convince us that the Germans were responsible for the systematic massacre of the Polish officers found in the mass grave at Katyn.

We discovered a guilty complacence toward (inevitable) misfortune and daily despair in a whole body of fiction that we read avidly, to tell the truth (especially my mother and I), in spite of the term "Jewish literature" by which we referred to it at home. I mention here a random selection of the books we blithely classified under that label, some of whose authors were certainly not Jewish. *Dusty Answer* by Rosamond Lehmann, *Tessa* by Margaret Kennedy, Kessel's *Crossroads*, Hardy's *Jude the Obscure*, the great trilogy by Jacob Wassermann (*Der Fall Maurizius, Etzel Andergast, Joseph Kerkhoven*), and *Rebecca* by Daphne Du Maurier. I think Louis-Ferdinand Céline was lucky enough to be officially recognized as a right-wing anti-Semite, otherwise *Voyage* (*Journey to the*

End of Night) and *Mort à crédit* (*Death on the Installment Plan*), which for me are still his two great books, would certainly have been tarred with the same brush—which would not, however, have stopped us from reading them over and over again with delight, quite the contrary . . .

Yet having reached this point in my story, I find it more and more difficult to go on saying "we" when speaking of the family ideology. I wanted to mention Kafka's novels here and immediately realized that I didn't read them until after the war, and by then I had changed. Of course we never stay the same, from one year to the next, one hour to the next. But the year 1945 represented a real break in my life. For my personal relations with order underwent a profound change after the Liberation, and especially after the Allied troops entered Germany, accompanied every day by monstrous revelations about the reality of the camps and the whole dark horror that was the hidden face of National Socialism. (For me the existence of gas chambers is not at issue, given that men, women, and children died by the millions, innocent of any crime except that of being Jews, Gypsies, or homosexuals.)

I myself came back from Germany at the end of July 1944 (or the beginning of August, I'm not quite sure), repatriated for reasons of health after a year of S.T.O. (Service du Travail Obligatoire) and a month in the hospital. But during my stay in Nuremberg I hadn't learned much about the real nature of the Nazi regime. Fischbach camp was actually a very ordinary labor camp where we were all cooped up together: Serbian peasants conscripted en masse, "voluntary" French workers, young people from Charente and Parisian students who had made the mistake of being born in 1922

93

(there was a group of about thirty students from the Agro and Grignon who, like everyone else, had become semiskilled workers in a war factory after trying in vain to find work in agriculture), as well as many other categories and nationalities; but it was an immense camp, and we only knew the inmates of three or four neighboring barracks in the same row as ours who used the same canteen and communal latrines.

Obviously it's hard to stand at an automatic lathe for seventy-two hours a week, especially when you're on night shift one week out of two; obviously it isn't pleasant or healthy to live mainly on rotten potatoes swimming in a greasy sauce; obviously it was cold in winter and the water often froze in the bottles at the foot of our bunks, whose mattresses were sacks of straw swarming with enormous fleas; obviously we had no protection from the regular nightly bombardments except the holes we dug on Sundays, as best we could, in the frozen, snow-covered ground. But many Germans were more or less in the same boat, not to mention those who were fighting on the Russian front.

And we weren't mistreated or penned behind concentration-camp barbed wire. There were watchtowers scattered around, but they were for scouting fires in the pine forests that covered most of the countryside. During the far too brief apprenticeship period, when we had a little more free time and weren't yet exhausted by the work, we could even go to concerts in town or dine at the village inn in the evening, or we could go for strolls in the country and visiting the small villages in the area (our permits as foreign workers authorized us to travel within a radius of one hundred kilometers of the factory, if only so we could get back to our lodgings, which were three-quarters of an hour away by train). It was the beginning of 1943, it was hot, the people were pleasant, there were very few air raids, the pine trees smelled wonderfully of resin and were posted with signs saying, "Only pyromaniacs smoke here," and we could go right up to the wild does who watched us with large, mild eyes—as it will be, they say, in the Kingdom of Heaven.

But even later, when winter came and our working conditions deteriorated, the imagery of order reigning over dear old Germany remained intact. Little blond children still smiled by the roadside; the public sidewalks were still clean and nature fair, whether green or white; the impeccable soldiers of the Wehrmacht still marched with a heavy tread, singing in unison in their deep voices; trains arrived on time; foremen carried on in dutiful drudgery; but if we did have to wait in a smoke-filled room in the main station for a convoy delayed by sabotage on the line—quickly repaired—the officers on leave (they too had tired faces under their flat, rigid helmets) would share their apples with the French students, telling them how much they loved Paris, Notre Dame, and *Pelléas*.

In fact the only disruption was caused by English or American planes, which with no visible effect on the war effort (the incendiary bombs seemed to prefer our modest barracks to the imposing M.A.N. factory) methodically destroyed the tidy medieval city and considerably disturbed what sleep was left to us in our new conscript life, making it all the more exhausting. And when I lay paralyzed on my mattress with acute rheumatoid arthritis, at the end of my tether, I was taken to an underground hospital in a region that had been spared (Ansbach), where the doctors and nurses looked after me in the normal way, often even with kindness.

In front of the Nuremberg station there was a huge poster painted in lurid colors, depicting scenes of crime and madness (fires, rapes, murders, massacres, etc.)— an apocalyptic vision with this caption in Gothic letters: "Victory or Bolshevik chaos!" Today more than ever we know that is not the case at all. It is not chaos that reigns in the U.S.S.R., quite the contrary. Under the Soviet regime too it is absolute order that breeds horror.

And suddenly everything falls apart. The upright generous soldiers, the neat pretty little nurses, the apples of friendship, the tame does and the children's fair smiles—it was all a hoax. Or rather, it only represented half the system, the half visible from the outside, the shopwindow, as it were; and now we were stupefied to discover the back of the shop, where demented soldiers silently slit the throats of children, nurses, and does (voiceless screams and mute laughter—the stuff of nightmares).

Then we remember a few clues that occasionally shocked us, fugitive cracks in the smooth polished surface of the shopwindow, quickly covered up by a reassuring "There's a war on, you know!"—which actually explained nothing. . . . In a bakery in Nuremberg, a sign just like any other (such as "Closed Mondays" or "Please Do Not Touch the Bread") calmly announced, "No Cakes Sold to Jews or Poles." Human beings were in effect divided into distinct categories that didn't have the same rights.

We ourselves didn't wear badges or distinguishing marks on our clothing (the administration contented itself with deducting in advance a considerable part of our wages under the heading "surtax on foreign workers," that is, "those who come and live here at our expense"), but the German Jews, as in France, wore a yellow star on their chests (there were few enough of these around in 1944, we know why), the Ukrainians were identified by the word *Ost* (an abbreviation of *Ostarbeiter*, "worker from the East") in white on a blue square, and the Poles, the dear Poles—whom the French always take to their hearts, for once unanimous—could be recognized by the letter P sewn on their clothes, which denied them the right to strudel and triangles of colored pastry topped with ersatz cream. . . . When one loves order, one classifies. And when one has classified, one sticks labels on. What could be more natural?

And then an image from the hospital in Ansbach. . . . I'm no longer in the tiny underground room crowded with the dying and helpless, too ill to go down to the shelters in case of an air-raid warning, where it was silent as a morgue and every morning a modest curtain was drawn around those who had died in the night (there was a rod around each bed for just this purpose, two meters from the floor). In a long, bright room with fifty iron beds lined up in two rows, one on the window side and the other against the blind wall, there's a surprisingly tall, big man just opposite me; he has the face of a peaceable beast and gives the impression of being strong as an ox, but he's probably in the last stages of tuberculosis, judging by his interminable cough and horrible bouts of spitting.

One day they come for him: four soldiers who obviously aren't nurses or doctors. The man refuses to move and begins to bellow loudly in his cavernous bass voice, interspersing words in Russian or a similar language. The nice nurses turn away, looking embarrassed, and explain to us that this patient is incurable and must be transferred to another hospital. Now on his feet, he is struggling feebly, still bawling like a beast being led to slaughter; he apparently knows very well what kind of hospital they mean. Those in charge dress him and finally drag him away as best as they can. They don't even come up to his shoulder. He seems to belong to a different species from his guards. The *Ost* badge is sewn onto his coat. . . . When one wants to order everything in a man's life, one must also take care to order his death.

While I was still being treated with aspirins in the Fischbach camp infirmary, some peasants from Charente trapped a doe in the snow. Too easy. And certainly not a very clever thing to do. In winter the forest rangers looked after the herd lovingly, counting them and bringing them bales of straw and hay. The tracks in the virgin snow—of victim and poacher—made the investigation a foregone conclusion, particularly since, like any proud hunter, this one had kept a foot as a trophy. I don't know what became of him, but I never saw him again in Fischbach.

But our Parisian male nurse, a serious, dedicated medical student, was accused of sheltering patients who were faking illness (since they were well enough to go hunting in the nearby forest), and in addition, of hiding their criminal activities (since he hadn't denounced the culprits). He was also taken away. He reappeared a few months later, just before I went back to France. He was so changed that I had trouble recognizing him: emaciated, hands trembling slightly, eyes sunk into gaping sockets and constantly filled with horror. He now spoke only rarely, hesitantly, and instantly fell silent when asked what had happened to him in the interim. He was like that English officer in a Kipling story who comes back from Srinagar after being held captive by the Russians. . . . To his friends who pressed him with questions, the former nurse finally conceded this one sentence: "I have known another kind of camp."

And even so, that was still a camp from which you could return. During the year 1945 we learned that others existed where the administration had arranged for admission with no return. But between the Fischbach camp and those of the Night and Fog there could doubtless be found all the intermediaries, methodically classified and indexed. A very minor detail struck me instantly, perhaps out of all proportion: they all had the same barracks, which all had the same beds. . . . Still more disquieting: the one where I myself lived had previously been used to house those who came to parade in the regime's grandiose rallies during the party congresses, and the oppressive, pompous constructions built for these occasions (in typical Hitlero-Stalinist style) still loomed a few kilometers away.

Although the family unit was as close-knit as ever—except for the fact that my sister, a recent graduate of Grignon, was now working as chief stockbreeder on a large farm in Seine-et-Marne—all the members of the clan certainly didn't react in the same way to the shock caused by the German defeat and the dramatic change of perspective on state systems appealing to order. For my mother and father the situation was as clear-cut as before, and there was no need to modify political choices. My mother quite simply refused to believe. As for my father, he calmly declared that if Germany had won, she could have laid all the war crimes she pleased at the door of her conquered enemies. International law is the law of the strongest. The loser is always in the wrong. The fact that Soviet Russia, already suspected of being far from guiltless, was simpering on the side of virtue could obviously justify such clichés. And naturally a few questions had to be asked about how useful those two bombs dropped at the last minute on Nagasaki and Hiroshima were to humanity.

When Paris was liberated, Papa was disgusted by the grotesque last-minute saraband of the French Forces of the Interior and by the pusillanimity of the good people who suddenly turned Gaullist and bellicose with the same enthusiasm they had recently displayed for Pétain and the armistice—like those girls, proletarian or bourgeois, who instantly offered their beds, sheets still damp, to the new conquering armies. There was also the gaucherie of the gum-chewing American GIs, which—at least in my father's eyes—formed a dramatic and unfortunate contrast to the military correctness of our occupiers, even in retreat.

I'm sure that all this made him feel as if he himself had just lost the war for the second time. Everything he detested was about to begin all over again, worse than ever: license, demagogy, personal profit, the parliamentary sham, "whipped-dog politics" (lying back and drifting with the current), and the collapse of France. And though he didn't launch into insults or jeremiads, I do remember this simple prophecy: "This time, children, we'll be lucky if we hang on to Corsica!"

He didn't harbor the same kind of resentment toward the Americans as he did toward the English; he even felt a vague sympathy for this distant people, perhaps dating from Lafayette and the shared victory against the English enemy. But the way the American air force had carelessly bombed our Breton and Norman towns and villages (the small city of Aunay-sur-Odon, five kilometers away, was razed to the ground "by mistake" the day after the Germans left, while the whole population was celebrating its new liberty) left him with the feeling that the army of the Reich had above all been conquered by a huge industrial machine; he forgot that four years earlier the panzer divisions and the Luftwaffe had played a similar role. Paradoxically, the German tanks were a credit to the courageous recovery of an industrious nation, whereas the tanks and bombers of the United States only proved the detestable power of money.

I was twenty-three years old then, but today I have the curious feeling that I was just emerging from childhood. Bretons are not known for being precocious. There were no showdowns or clashes at home, where I was living again after my Bavarian interlude. Still, without always consciously realizing it, I saw things differently from then on. While fully understanding my parents' reactions, I now found it impossible to agree with them on certain crucial points.

In particular, a respect for order at all cost now made me profoundly suspicious, to say the least. We'd just seen where that got us. If you had to accept the other side of the coin as well, the price was definitely too high. For I don't believe that Hitler and Stalin were accidents of history: even if they were clinically insane, they in fact represented the logical conclusion of the systems they incarnated. And if we really have to choose between that and disorder, there's no doubt I would choose disorder.

However, I'm not saying that traumatized as I was, I instantly relinquished the ideological need for order and classification. This need is very much alive in all of us, side by side with the desire for freedom—its opposite—and everyone has that too. These two opposing forces within us are in constant interaction, both in our conscious mind and in the depths of our unconscious. It's simply a matter of proportion, and human beings differ according to the particular form this tortuous duality takes within each individual. My father himself seems to have been a typical example of this insoluble inner contradiction: sensitive individualist yet profascist on occasion, anarchist to the core yet staunch supporter of absolute monarchy ruling by divine right (tempered by regicide), loyal Pétainist happy to replace the republic's "Liberty, Equality, Fraternity," with the slogan of the new order, "Work, Family, Nation," yet instinctively hostile to regimentation of any kind.

And so within me this proportion was changing: the two irreconcilable forces no longer worked the same way as before, and the new tension that resulted could no longer be expressed in such simple positions. There was no question of replacing the Institut de la Statistique with terrorist action, nor even leftist agitation. But I was quite naturally drawn to problematic experimentation

101

with fiction and its contradictions (I stress once more that this is how I see my adventure today) as the most promising arena in which to act out this permanent imbalance: the fight to the death between order and freedom, the insoluble conflict between rational classification and subversion, otherwise known as disorder.

Throughout the fifties orthodox leftists strongly reproached me because my writing was "disengaged" and even blamed me for its "demoralizing influence on the young." But in the first place, I had seen the face of death and didn't necessarily feel I was in the best position to give my fellow citizens public moral lessons on institutions and their possible transformation (revolutionary or reformist); I had no inclination to imitate my numerous ex-Stalinist colleagues who, in the name of their own mistakes (usually confessed with tongue in cheek), don't hesitate to indoctrinate us all over again. But there's more to it. Just as one could hardly have stayed in the French Communist Party for twenty long years (long because strewn with recurring traps and bitter pills) without a steadfast militance, a partisan spirit ready to swallow anything, so I think I see in myself a very ancient refusal of all militant faith, an *a fortiori* refusal of *engagement* as Sartre defined it.

During the period of my adolescent submission to codes of moral order and the political right, I'm afraid I already felt more or less an amateur, a dilettante. Even my nationalism at the time—the most respectable of the traditional right-wing attributes—seems to have been somewhat suspect. My mother experienced things much more intensely, discussed everything passionately, and I remember her reproaching me at the beginning of the war for seeming unconcerned about the Germans' lightning advance into Poland. I justified myself, but in a sense she was right. For in June 1940 I certainly was affected by the dramatic rout of our troops, but as if from behind a pane of glass.

We had been living at Kerangoff since the general mobilization and hadn't gone back to Paris for the beginning of the autumn term because there were no more math classes at Lycée Buffon (or anywhere else in Paris). Fortunately Maman was well again since she'd been "radio-ed" (my father's expression, which we all immediately adopted: the idiolects of small, exclusive clans require a systematic resort to invented words and twisted meanings). And although she still spent part of the night reading the papers Papa sent on from Paris, the rest of the time she was very busy running and feeding the whole household, which included, besides Grandmother, Godmother (who did the shopping), my sister and me, our two first cousins (refugees from the lycée in Brest, like us), and a friend of our age who was boarding with us.

(After the war our mother's often dormant energies found a new outlet, and she flourished once more at Kerangoff: she single-handedly conceived and supervised the complete reconstruction of the large family house, which had been almost totally demolished by Allied bombing—"a one-hundred-percent disaster," according to local officials. Maman said that she was much happier with large undertakings than with petty daily tasks.)

No, I wasn't indifferent, that's not at all what I remember. But I doubtless felt deep down that it wasn't me who was losing the battle. For ages I'd thought that our governments were puppets, our generals were inept, and our army had been wrecked by the Popular Front, so I did have trouble suddenly identifying with a France so utterly discredited. I was simply condemned to accept what others had been preparing for me for a long time now. Of course I can't claim to have attempted any move in the other direction; but at seventeen what could I have done? The stupidly reassuring news broadcast by the authorities added further to this feeling of impotence and abandonment. We were fed lies like children.

And perhaps my firm conviction that I belonged to a very small group, absolutely separate from the masses, a belief carried to extremes in the clan ideology (we Robbe-Grillets were accused of considering the rest of the world a bunch of imbeciles), was hardly conducive to the sudden national solidarity demanded of me. Finally, there was our distance from the battlefields. This end of Finistère was miles and miles from the Vistula. The Rhine, the Meuse, and the Somme were scarcely much closer. I lived in another world. I worked hard at school ("top of the class," according to my report card— but I always loved learning and still do), I did my homework conscientiously, I did well on exams. . . . I was a demilitarized zone, a solitary unofficial observer, forgotten in an open city . . .

The war broke in on us brutally, in an unexpected form: Papa, left at the garden gate in broad daylight by a military driver in a battered car crudely repainted a drab gray so it would be less of a mark for enemy aircraft, but nevertheless pocked with holes from the spray of Stuka machine guns. Papa was pale, and his usual nervousness was much more pronounced than usual. He told us what had happened in short, dry, neutral sentences, as briefly as possible.

Having burned the useless records of our armaments in the courtyard of the ministry, he had set out in a convoy going south, soon lost in the flood of an exodus in which neither civilians nor soldiers knew what they were advancing toward. The bridges over the Loire had been destroyed, and they had to find another farther to the west. Feeling that he was of no use in the midst of this debacle and was merely adding to the confusion, he decided to go back to Brest, to the only beings he felt responsible for—which was relatively easy since those roads were much less crowded with fugitives. Desertion of his post? But he no longer had a post! Anyway, our father had once declared that he was capable of anything, even murder, to protect his own family.

That day he also said that the war was lost, irretrievably, that we had no matériel, no army, no allies, no recourses of any kind. . . . At times he could hardly bring out the words—perhaps because his throat was constricted with anguish, or the suppressed tears of defeat, or the emotion of actually finding us all again. My mother kept repeating, "Are you sure?" She didn't want to believe that it was all over, that there was no protest possible, no miracle to hope for. . . . She wept with indignation. . . . The driver went off in his battered car to try to find his own family across the German lines. No wonder Marshal Pétain seemed like a guiding light, in the midst of such a disaster.

And so we had the Occupation: omnipresent but with no commotion, functioning smoothly, and fairly unobtrusive from the outside, except for a few parades with blaring music, which were considered as slightly comical if anything. The German soldiers were polite, young, smiling; they gave the impression of being serious, full of goodwill, almost ingratiating, as if they wanted to apologize for having entered our peaceful territory uninvited. They radiated discipline and neatness. (The very rare rapists and looters had instantly been punished harshly by their superiors.) Whether they wore green or black, these tall blond boys who drank water and sang in unison were at first regarded as some kind of strange beast. On a large propaganda poster (which had replaced Paul Reynaud's "We will conquer because we are the strongest") one of them was helping a little girl across the street, holding her hand; the caption read, "Trust the German soldier." Certainly in 1940–41 that picture and text didn't seem a shocking provocation. If you didn't live through that time, it's difficult to see that Vercors's famous novel, *Le silence de la mer*, printed clandestinely by Editions de Minuit, was a novel of resistance. People kept saying, "At least they're well behaved." France deep down heaved a sigh of relief. And doubtless, when all's said and done, being out of the action suited me quite well too. We weren't on one side or the other anymore, we had got rid of the English yet had no real commitment to the Germans. Thanks to the Marshal, we had suddenly, miraculously become a neutral country, like Switzerland. . . . Better still: disarmed! It was as if our eventual allegiance to one camp or the other had been put in parentheses; even our most impassioned views were now merely a subject for friendly discussion with the family, in the corner café, or in bittersweet exchanges with cantankerous neighbors.

I could calmly go on being a disinterested amateur, a witness on unpaid leave. The Occupation was a bit like the "phony war": terrible things were going on all over the world that were likely to be of vital importance for our future, but for the time being we were excluded. We only heard about them from a distance, through newspapers that mostly had to be read between the lines, and from the radio, which didn't even disguise its partisan and propagandistic character. Pétain's "wait and see" policy (for which the real collaborators roundly reproached him) looked like political wisdom and national vocation at one and the same time.

What else was there to do? Carry on the fight courageously, underground or by crossing the Channel to help England deliver us one day? Join the bitter European crusade against the Communist hydra? I knew a very few boys who threw themselves into the fray in one or the other of these causes. They were seen more as kids looking for a good fight than as heroes. As one of Beckett's characters would say, "Let's not do anything, it's safer!"

The family had returned to Paris. I spent two years studying for the Agro exams at Lycée Saint-Louis in the same class as my sister and got in with a very good grade in the autumn of 1942. As Brest was off limits, we spent our summers at Guingamp with our aunt Mathilde Canu, who taught arithmetic in a school in the town. All around was woodland, the old Breton earth where oaks and ferns grew. One memory among others: the small street where we lived led to the cemetery; a detachment of verdigris soldiers passes under our window and disappears in that direction; the first six are carrying a coffin on their shoulders, the others are lumbering along behind, their heavy boots thudding on the uneven, glistening cobblestones. These are no longer the fine young men of the invasion, but reservists, doubtless ill equipped to endure the hardships of the Eastern Front. They're singing in unison "I had a comrade . . ." in a slow, utterly despairing bass. A fine drizzle is falling on the straggling column as it makes its way down the middle of the street, falling over the whole town and adding its own Celtic note to the nostalgia of the old song from beyond the Rhine in memory of dead companions.

The capital wasn't very cheery either; it too was empty of cars and silent, which gave it a new beauty. And it couldn't be said that the German troops were crowding it on patrol or as tourists: obviously they had better things to do. The Parisian pedestrian enjoyed a sort of freedom in this vacuum: the freedom of desert expanses, or of abandon, or of sleep. We went for long, aimless strolls through the phantom city. Once my father and I pushed a rented wheelbarrow from one end of town to the other to bring back a providential sack of coal. In winter the cold was a problem, on top of the constant scarcity of food, and worries about prosaic essentials often took precedence over everything else. Papa devoted himself body and soul to the material support of the clan.

Once I got into the Agro and was at last certain of completing my long, costly studies, I worked a little less enthusiastically, or rather, I chose the subjects I was interested in (plant biology, genetics, biochemistry, geology . . .), completely neglecting the others (agricultural mechanization, rural engineering, industrial technology). I went to a lot of concerts and to the opera. There were certainly many German officers there, and they were even in the majority in the box seats of some famous concert halls, particularly the Palais Garnier. But they didn't bother me: they were a very quiet audience, almost invisible in their stiff uniforms, and didn't we all appreciate the same music—Bach, Beethoven, Wagner, Debussy, Ravel? In any case, their seats were much too expensive for my modest budget: paradoxically, I was the one looking down on them from on high.

There were "circles" at the Institut Agronomique, small groups of students with the same interests: bridge, chess, riding, dancing. With a few friends, including the future painter Bernard Dufour, we'd started the Agro Music Circle, but as most of its members were openly Pétainist, our classmates, who pretended to consider us shocking collaborators, called us—quite amicably—the "K group." Since the entry of the United States into the war and the German difficulties on the Eastern front, the Gaullists had increased in number. But all that remained in the realm of speculation and didn't cause any animosity or real division between the opposed factions.

One day, however, in a mischievous mood (I always enjoyed provoking my fellow students), I had swiped a bundle of papers two "anglophile" students were collating with a mysterious air in the last row of the lecture hall. Amazement: they were detailed plans for the defense of Paris! When I saw their sudden anxiety, I realized that they were playing at the Resistance more actively—if not more effectively—than I'd thought. I was even more surprised when I realized they were afraid that I'd denounce them. I immediately gave the compromising papers back. This gesture—quite natural, I thought—earned me a similar indulgence in the autumn of 1944, in the middle of the hysterical purges in the second and last year of our studies, when I was back again with my classmates who had been in the maquis or simply in hiding.

At the end of spring 1943, all students born in 1922 were called up for S.T.O., supposedly instead of military service, from which the "class of '42" had been exempted, but with no possibility of deferment even for those just a few months from graduation. This civilian mobilization took place under the pretext of "relieving" our soldiers: we were going to work in Germany to replace prisoners of war who, thanks to us, could return home after three years in captivity.

Did we believe this? We half believed it. Anyway, we were suckers. But the old marshal needed us. In the papers you saw edifying photos of families shedding tears of happiness, greeting a father or husband who had returned after such a long absence. Besides, we were promised agricultural work, which was what a large number of the liberated prisoners had been doing. We could therefore think of this compulsory stay as a sort of practical training, like the stint we'd done the year before in "rural civic service" on French farms between entrance exams and the beginning of the course. The director of the Institut Agronomique came to the main lecture hall in person to address the two classes assembled for the occasion and urge us to go. I remember his peroration: "Go to Germany, young people, you will get to know a great country." At the time of the Liberation he'd been a longstanding member of the Resistance and therefore had no trouble keeping his job. And without the least embarrassment he welcomed us back to the school with an appropriate speech.

Of course the K group was easily persuaded to go. But so were many others. The ones who got out of it were mainly those who took advantage of close rural ties and could hope to find conditions more favorable to a semi-clandestine existence in the provinces. In exchange for our obedience to the call, we who had enlisted received a train ticket to Bavaria, a new pair of galoshes, a tin of sardines in oil, and a ticket to go hear Edith Piaf in a huge Parisian theater. . . . We were setting off to relieve the prisoners, Piaf was singing for us, Pétain was smiling under his white moustache. . . . I put on the galoshes, gave the sardines to my mother, and listened gravely to Edith Piaf, a tiny, touching figure in the far distance, facing rows and rows of seats filled with departing labor conscripts.

Soon after, along with other students from the Agro and Grignon, I found myself in Nuremberg, city of Hans Sachs and the Meistersingers, working as a lathe operator in a heavy armaments factory that specialized in the manufacture of the famous Panther tanks. But our two-month apprenticeship was almost like a vacation. As work didn't begin for the novices till midday, we had our mornings free to wander in the pine forests and meadows near the camp. Thanks to the provisions our families managed to send we played at cooking our lunch on small stoves that we improvised outside the barracks. At the factory, the theory classes consisted of inculcating the rudiments of mathematics, which was obviously more important for our Yugoslav comrades, whose knowledge of the subject wasn't nearly so extensive as that of trained engineering students. Anyway, our instructor, who was Turkish (and whose supposed linguistic prowess must have been responsible for the apparently bizarre mélange that comprised our class), spoke to us in so strange a language—directly modeled on German grammatical structures, with a vocabulary largely consisting of German words more or less gallicized—that we weren't always able to tell when he switched from French to Serbo-Croatian. Luckily some of the same phrases came up every day, and we finally got their gist.

Here, for example, is the ritual opening of any instruction on using an automatic lathe: "The first, normal, what do you do? So, gentlemen, receive you material in *patin-foutre* . . ."—that is, you begin by putting the part into the mandrel. The mandrel is called *Patten-Futter* in German; as for the verb "to receive," *bekommen*, which is an all-purpose word in colloquial speech, rather like the American "to check" our teacher's use of it was as liberal as his vocabulary was limited.

But before long, having had enough of our sniggering incomprehension, he would decide to address himself to the Serbian half of his audience. The key phrase informing us that the "French" class had just ended was, "So, gentlemen, get on with you private work," which meant we were now free to write to our families undisturbed. (My long, detailed letters must also be packed away in the low-beamed attic at Kerangoff— favorite territory for us children when it rained—along with the tender, illegible daily reports my father wrote to my mother during their temporary separations, seasonal or accidental, as well as the older, rarer letters— the mail ships weren't very frequent at the end of the last century—sent by Grandfather Canu from China, Tonkin, or Valparaiso.)

Immediately thereafter, the signal *"Akotomaserbé"* woke up the other side of the room; but we could tell that this was yet another mispronunciation of our language: *"Ecoutez-moi, Serbes!"* Never being sure of really understanding what was going on, constantly interpreting, accepting guesswork, uncertainty, ambiguity, and gaps in communication as your normal relation with the world, was now part of our life, and also, in a sense,

111

of its exotic attraction. In short, this was my first vacation abroad, since my past trips to the Swiss border had involved very little linguistic disorientation.

For our practical training with the metalworking tools or on the machines, our foreman was so benevolent and blasé that he agreed with a helpless smile to punch out for Dufour and me when we wanted to leave the factory early in order not to miss the beginning of a concert. *"Franzoz, grosse Lump!"* he concluded philosophically, which gave me the chance in particular to hear all of Beethoven's sonatas for piano and cello at the Katherinenkirche, a small white and gold baroque church, and a ravishing setting for chamber music.

I really had the feeling—a mixture of flippancy, distance, and suspense—that I was just a tourist. Handling files, the vise, the lathe, or the drilling machine seemed like a game to me, as I love manual labor, and for my own amusement I even began to make a steel chess set, which I didn't finish, alas, like so many other things. A few weeks later, when I was on the assembly line, obeying forced rhythms that left no time for rest or daydreaming, standing every day at my lathe for two shifts of five and a half hours at a stretch, grinding the monstrous crankshafts of the tanks (which were so heavy they had to be lifted by an electric hoist) within five hundredths of a millimeter—with no scope for deviation or imagination—my life had certainly changed, abruptly and completely, but I still felt convinced I was only a tourist.

The life of a semiskilled worker is a hopeless one, and yet at no time did I despair: I was only passing through and had no real past or future link with this factory; I was aimless, there by chance, by mistake, as it were. And on Saturday evening, when a small poster with a swastika appeared above the time clock to inform us

that we had to work on Sunday, for the German Fatherland, the war effort, the final victory, etc., I managed
after a fashion to translate the text up to the words in
bold type—"Your Führer needs you!"—without feeling in the least involved. Of course I'd have to work all
the next day like my comrades on the assembly line,
Bavarians, Swabians, Franconians, but unlike them—
and I could see the difference in their drawn faces—I
didn't feel in any way committed to the business because I should never have been doing this job: I wasn't a
real worker, I wasn't German, he wasn't my Führer, and
in any case this eventual victory wouldn't be mine either.

I saw quite a few comrades around me who certainly
seemed better equipped to identify with the improvised
role they were made to play, sometimes even professed
Gaullists, working for the enemy war effort with a conviction I totally lacked, which made it easier for me to
gauge the fundamental *strangeness* of my own relation to
the world, doubtless more serious than the simple fact of
expatriation. With no thought of sabotage, without the
slightest ill will, I never managed to meet the prescribed
quota correctly (I'm good with my hands but not with
machines), while the others became real precision
grinders or drill operators or what have you in a matter
of days.

Once, when I was in the infirmary reveling in one of
the early works of Ilya Ehrenburg, *Julio Jurenito* (the
stock of discarded books that made up the camp's
French library seemed to come primarily from the Nazi
auto-da-fé), I offered to show a young French peasant,
who was due to be sent back to work because he was
better, how to raise the thermometer readings by gently
rubbing the mercury bulb with a woolen sock. But the
boy answered that he preferred to get back to his machine because of "the wife and kids starving to death in
La Roche, Indre-et-Loire"—a doubly absurd pretext
since the social security system, which was quite good

113

for its time, would have paid him the same wages while he was ill, and since, as I heard later, he didn't have a wife or children. He was hoping for the Allied landing even as he clung to his position as a German worker. He missed his punch press.

By contrast, the feeling of exteriority, almost of extra-territoriality, that I experienced so strongly (remaining on the outside, being there by accident, as the result of a misunderstanding more amusing than tragic) stayed with me even at night when the air-raid sirens, immediately followed by the dull roar of bombers, tore us out of our precious sleep and made us leap from our bunks and flee the barracks, some of which would soon go up in flames. The sky would be bright with clusters of incandescent flares drifting slowly down toward us (to light up targets?), diffusing a bright pink glow punctuated by short white bursts from the antiaircraft guns, while the burning pine forests ("Only pyromaniacs smoke here!") stained large patches of the horizon a smoky orange.

Doubtless the fact that we weren't in town heightened the theatrical quality of the scene. The camp was strewn with signal flares that went off on the ground like dud fireworks. And even when we heard the big bombs whining and threw ourselves down on the grass to wait for the muffled crash of the final explosion, imagining it to be right beside us because the earth was trembling so violently, once again, despite the danger, it was as if the fact that I was there by mistake played a decisive part in my safety: I was not at war with these planes, their bombs weren't aimed at me, and even if I were to be killed I would still be an extra on the casualty lists—one corpse too many, a phantom metalworker accidentally entered in the production statistics.

Maybe it was only in the morning, back in the damaged city, that I felt as if I'd lost something, a part of myself gone forever, or at least I felt a pained sympathy—although useless, impotent, and therefore of no practical help—in front of the shapeless ruins of a pretty baroque church that had been lovingly maintained for centuries, or beside the clear waters of the Pegnitz, facing the charred remains of big wooden houses with flowered balconies dating from the Middle Ages. Every night a little piece of old Europe was disappearing in dust and smoke. . . . But isn't nostalgia for ruins—even recent ones—one of the traditional ingredients of the journey into the unknown?

And again it's that sensation of being an isolated visitor, protected behind a pane of glass, that I experience a few years later at the camp at Divotino, in the green hills of Bulgaria, amid fields of corn and tall sunflowers. I'm with Daniel Boulanger (whom I'd met in Prague the month before at a huge phony congress of so-called democratic youth) and Claude Ollier (whom I knew in Nuremberg in the summer of 1943); all three of us are volunteers in the "International Reconstruction Brigade." This time I'm wielding a pick and shovel on the future track of the Pernik-Voloviek railway. After I came back, in a text published about 1950 in an engineering magazine and reprinted in 1978 in the journal *Obliques*, I wrote about the utter absurdity of the work done on that site, the air of impenetrable mystery surrounding the recruitment of the young Bulgarian members of the "brigade," the rambling Marxist-Leninist propaganda speeches (in favor of peace, of course, and friendship among nations) punctuated by our chanting in unison the names of the heroes—"Stalin! Thorez! Tito! Dimitrov!"—until we burst into uncontrollable laughter, and the widening gulf in the French delegation between the true militant Communists and the others. Whether on the right or the left, my attempts at engagement certainly didn't agree with me.

In the same issue of *Obliques*, François Jost collected

evidence (photos, press clippings, quotations from books, etc.) on another biographical episode where I am once more distinctly (abnormally?) distanced from an event—an extremely dramatic one—that I'm in the midst of experiencing: a plane crash. I was with my wife on the first Air France Boeing 707 to crash: the Paris-Tokyo flight that went down during takeoff after the Hamburg stopover. This was in the early days of polar flights, in the summer of 1961.

A journalist from Agence France-Presse questioned me by phone at the Atlantic Hotel, where the uninjured passengers who wished to continue their journey on the next long-distance flight were staying. I reported as accurately as I could what I had just witnessed from my window seat in the tail of the plane, which gave me a clear view: the plane does not taxi down the center of the runway, the grassy shoulder on the left comes closer and closer as we keep on going, the wing dips suddenly on that side, one of the engines hits the ground and catches fire, the plane tilts in the opposite direction, tearing off the landing gear and a second engine, but still keeps moving on its belly over the bumpy ground, etc.

The remains of the fuselage, cut into three sections, come to a halt in a Z shape. Flames at least twenty meters high burst from the fuel tanks. Catherine and I, both sitting in the tail of the plane, find ourselves without a scratch, half buried in a piece of the cabin. Stupidly, I stop to look for her handbag—although there's nothing of value in it—among the seats, most of which have been torn loose, while the stewardesses outside are yelling, "Run! It's going to explode!" But the Japanese, hurrying across the sticky ground in their socks, through fragments and debris, nevertheless turn around many times to the blazing wreckage to take the photographs that will constitute the indisputable high point of their trip to Europe.

A little later, while the ambulance men are still freeing the seriously injured (no one was killed, as the plane was almost empty and all the seats at the points where it broke up happened to be empty), when the firemen are still not sure that they've put out all the flames (the plane didn't explode in the end) and thick black smoke is still gushing out, swirling above the thickly spread dry ice, a small Air France van pulls up right alongside the plane, a painter in white overalls gets out, very professional, leans his extension ladder against the shattered fuselage, climbs up with his materials, and calmly begins to paint out the famous Air France seahorse. An expert could probably recognize the remnants of the Boeing, but all 707s look alike, and none of the passengers who are taking off on the runway, staring goggle-eyed at the disturbing remains, need know to whom this one belonged.

Painter, firemen, ambulances. . . . Yet another car arrived on the scene, one of the first to make its way across the barely navigable ground, the so-called rescue vehicle: a blue-gray van, entirely covered inside with shelves full of brandy glasses. . . . The first-aid bartender was trembling so violently from shock himself that he spilled half his cognac. . . . One more image that recurs insistently: the crazy slope we had to climb after we got through the wide open door, in order to get out of the hole we were buried in, where Catherine's high-heeled shoes were left behind . . .

My reporter on the other end of the line doubtless considers me singularly lacking in a flair for the sensational: my account quite rightly seems to him objective enough but somewhat dull, whereas he has to make the accident as dramatic as possible. So he doesn't hesitate to put words into my mouth for tomorrow's press release, which will be wired to all the France-Presse dailies: a totally different version crammed with grandiloquent metaphors and stereotyped emotion. I read this two days later in Japan and am if anything amused. But by the end of the week my story, taking up a whole page in *L'Express*, has turned into a so-called literary scandal. Despite the article's trumped-up tone, the author obviously really thinks that this time I've been unmasked: my alleged account (which he pretends to believe is authentic, although he himself has been a reporter for many years on a magazine with a huge circulation and therefore knows the unscrupulous practices of the profession) proves that my writing as a novelist is contrived, fraudulent, since under the influence of fear I suddenly start talking like everyone else and "purely and simply tell the story of the crash"!

And here's what "purely and simply" is: "With an infernal roar the plane left the runway and began churning up the field like a giant plough," etc. Even among the staff of *L'Express* I can't imagine anyone who would speak like that in everyday life, even after surviving a plane crash. But the most amusing repercussion was the appearance in the bookshops several months later of *L'Oeuvre ouverte*, a fascinating essay on modern literature in which Umberto Eco, using arguments that were otherwise extremely cogent (the language of the writer, he says, is different from the language he uses for daily communication), defends me in particular against the sarcastic pamphleteer—thus giving credence to my authorship of the ravings published by A.F.P., as well as to the violent agitation that must have caused me to utter them.

I am dwelling here on the successive stages of this adventure first in order to point out once more that what we have inherited from the vile Zola is considered by the general public and its official spokesmen the most natural way of speaking and writing. But I also want to examine my actual reactions at the time of this abortive takeoff. On the one hand, I'm sure that I was alert enough behind my windowpane to follow the different stages of the accident second by second. On the other hand, I maintain that everything happened so fast that there was no time to be afraid. But Catherine, who was sitting two or three rows up and wasn't right next to a window, preferring a book to the view, says that on the contrary such a series of shocks lasts interminably and that the fear she experienced during those long moments haunted her for many years to come.

In fact, after agreeing—probably because of the tranquilizers they gave her—to set off again the next day for Tokyo by air (we didn't have time to take the Trans-Siberian Express because we had to be back for the Venice Film Festival, where *Marienbad*'s fate was to be decided—this was the film's last chance), and after returning with me to Rome by easy stages via Hong Kong (shaken up by an ill-timed typhoon over the China sea), Bangkok, Delhi, and Teheran (where all her paternal family lived), getting more and more frightened with each successive flight, even when the plane was as motionless—like Zeno's arrow—as the smoothest of Paris metros, she managed to communicate her anxiety to me by osmosis, and she had to give up air travel for ten years, which gave us the opportunity to range over the Old and New Worlds by rail, as well as to cross the oceans of North and South on luxurious liners that are now extinct.

During one of our last New York–Cherbourg crossings aboard the mythical but already commercial *Queen Elizabeth II*, there was an incident that reproduced yet again the same thought-provoking elements: danger, instant spectacle, journalists' evident disappointment in the face of any account lacking pathos, hyperbolic distortions of a story dramatized to titillate the masses. We're at sea, Catherine, my sister Anne-Lise, and I, on the third day of our crossing, roughly halfway between America and the French coast. We emerge from the cinema, a huge auditorium worthy of the Champs-Elysées, where we've just seen (in English, which none of us understands) a film in which an airliner gets into serious difficulties in midflight; I don't remember the details. It's the middle of the afternoon, and we take one of the big elevators that serves eleven or twelve decks and go up to the top deck to get some air.

The ship is motionless; we don't know why, but we do know this is odd. The lifeboats are ready at emergency stations: hoisted out over the water in their davits as if about to be lowered for an abandon-ship exercise. A few dozen sailors are bustling around them. They're all wearing life jackets and sou'westers, like Newfoundland fishermen in a storm. The sky's overcast, lowering. The ocean's as calm as it can be in the middle of the North Atlantic. People are strolling about, vaguely anxious, trading conjectures in different languages.

Various rumors run rife, and soon an official announcement from the captain informs us that there may be bombs on board, no one knows where, planted by terrorists who are demanding an enormous ransom from Cunard and threatening to blow up the whole ship if their terms aren't met; we are waiting for a bomb squad that's on its way from England to defuse the bombs. All the passengers dash to their cabins, only to rush back with movie cameras and photographic equipment, which they'd run off to fetch without a moment's delay: what a piece of luck! They'll be able to film the arrival of the military aircraft, the dropping of the frogmen and bomb-disposal equipment, and maybe even— if their luck holds—the explosion, the shipwreck, their own death . . .

The beginning of the operation fulfills their expectations. Three planes emerge from the clouds and dive several times in the direction of the liner, one after the other, doubtless to plot its exact position. Then they drop four men in black wetsuits, and also a number of containers, all harnessed to orange parachutes. Three of the lifeboats, launched with their crews, pick them up with no trouble, although from the promenade deck they're so far away that we can hardly make out the details of this rescue in heavy seas.

For some eight hours the immense *Q.E. II*—her engines still turned off—is systematically inspected with the most advanced equipment, from top to bottom, above, below, inside. In the middle of the night, a new announcement from the captain finally informs us that the search has proved vain, that in any case nothing has been found near the vital organs of the ship, and that we can therefore continue on our way; if it does turn out that there are bombs on board, they can only be of a relatively low explosive power and must be hidden in the cabins (which haven't been searched), so that if there is an explosion it won't interfere with the smooth sailing of the ship. It's hard to tell whether this last detail is an example of the British sense of humor. Anyway, the rest of the crossing was spent celebrating in honor of the "good fellows" who had risked their lives to save us.

At Cherbourg, the first port of call, all the television networks in Europe and America, as well as all the daily and weekly papers and the radio stations, etc., are there to welcome us. The reporters mob us but are visibly disappointed by our accounts of the drama: no, no one panicked; yes, people took photos; no, we weren't really frightened, we continued eating and drinking, watching adventure films, playing jackpot and lotto; yes, all things considered, we actually enjoyed ourselves. . . . But in front of the mass media in full deployment, filming us on all sides and hounding us with questions, we really do feel that we're not rising to the occasion. Some of our interviewers are almost angry: for two cents they'd happily blame us for not having been blown to pieces and gone down with the ship, singing in unison, "Nearer, my God, to Thee, nearer to Thee . . ."

Even in Hamburg, I'd ended up feeling guilty when my journalist, who was getting more and more irritated on the other end of the line, finally abandoned his pose of feigned compassion and accused me outright of not being sufficiently moved by the crash. I remember one detail in particular: he really hoped that I had "lost all my manuscripts" in the disaster. That, at least, in the absence of charred bodies or survivors maddened by shock, might make an acceptable scoop: imagine the despair throughout the land of France, from château to humble cottage, when they learned that the only draft of *L'Immortelle* and all the preliminary notes for *La Maison de rendez-vous* had just gone up in flames forever with one hundred thousand liters of kerosene . . .

As I was endeavoring to get across to him that a writer doesn't usually travel with those kinds of things, which are precious, cumbersome, and heavy, especially when he's going to the other side of the world for initial talks on a film project, my enraged interlocutor, at his wits' end, hurled at me, "So you really don't give a damn that all your luggage was burned to a crisp!"

In order to calm him down, I was then forced to betray a small personal secret, a meager tidbit: unbeknownst to Catherine, I had in my luggage a pretty gold necklace that I was going to give her on the anniversary of our meeting on the Orient Express going to Istanbul, exactly ten years ago on August 4, that is, less than a week after the abortive takeoff in which we had just nearly died together.

Ten years already. Thirty-three today. . . . Summer 1951, stuck on page 40 of *Les Gommes*, I had left Brest on impulse after reading an ad in *Combat* for a (very cheap) student trip to Turkey. Old Flaubertian mirage of escape to the Orient, where time has suddenly stopped. . . . Wallas, puzzling over the stupid riddle of the Sphinx, was waiting beside the troubled waters of his canal for the drawbridge to close again . . . waiting for days, for centuries. . . . Immemorial ruins bathed in the bright sun of Asia Minor; shadows cast by Sinan's minarets on rough cobbled esplanades where a solitary watchman, wrapped in his caftan, squats meditating against a pillar circled with bronze; beaches dreaming under fig trees beside the still, limpid Sea of Marmara; caïques sailing up the Golden Horn through the lengthening rays of the setting sun; the main street of Pera already lit by signs for dancing girls in the soft twilight and the floods of silent men in dark robes; the Galatasaray lycée where sugary, nostalgic melodies *alla turca* throbbed, lulling us to sleep in the big white marble dormitories; the innumerable little steamers with their gay plumes of black smoke, crisscrossing the Bosporus in the pale morning light with their motionless passengers wearing fezzes and heavy moustaches, their bundles wrapped in carpets, their sheep and itinerant tea vendors; the melancholy cry of the yoghurt sellers, the smell of grilled fish, and the peach ices that Catherine lived on almost exclusively . . .

She looked so young then that everyone thought she was still a child. Thirteen years old, "O Romeo, Juliet's age!" And people took her for my daughter, while she was searching for traces of her real father, who had survived the Armenian massacres as a small boy, clambering nimbly through the rustic streets of Kadiköy and Usküdar. . . . The necklace lost in the Boeing's hold commemorated all that.

I had spent weeks choosing it lovingly before we left, and now it would never be offered to the young girl of my dreams, trifling sentimental treasure buried forever between bittersweet memory and oblivion. But in *L'Express* the next week, my guilty secret had become: and when a writer of the New Novel loses all his luggage, it's not his manuscripts reduced to cinders that he laments, it's "his wife's jewelry"!

In the end, against all expectations, the beautiful new suitcases I also bought for this trip were returned to us a few hours later, hardly battered, in a pile of miscellaneous objects that had fallen out of more fragile baggage. On the other hand, the film co-production that we were on our way to Japan to discuss never got past the shooting script, since the rich Japanese Hollywood-style company that had hired me at great expense certainly didn't have the slightest idea of the unorthodox nature of the narrative structures I'd been constructing for several years now. These people had only called on me as the result of a total misunderstanding that was fostered for obscure reasons by a French backer and went on for a whole six months.

However, a few months later a big-budget film was made about the spectacular ransom of the *Q.E. II*. The French version was called *Terreur sur le Britannic*. The ominous, imposing sound "-itanic" alone already gives the clue: the greatest liner in the world keeling over after a fatal collision. The captain was none other than Omar Sharif, whose Anglo-Saxon looks are obviously somewhat debatable, and he had an amorous intrigue with a beautiful blonde in first class, married to someone else, naturally. Terrorist threats in midocean, air-sea rescue teams arriving posthaste from England, the company's equivocations, passengers mastering their distress (no question of taking photos), tense silences and glances, etc.

But the parachute drop of frogmen and equipment took place in a violent storm, which is much more commercial, and several sailors were swept off the gangways or buffeted in the foam as they hoisted the precious crates aboard big motor launches bobbing on the crest of thirty-foot waves. And this time there "really" were bombs hidden in the sophisticated bowels of the ship. The first even caused serious damage when they exploded, despite the skill and courage of the glorious bomb squad. The final catastrophe was only averted in the nick of time, after the obligatory hundred minutes of running time. But Omar Sharif, toughened by his ordeal, stiffened his upper lip and resolved henceforth to leave the pretty passengers to their husbands.

Among the real details of our adventure, one of the most noteworthy, which did spell potential tragedy at the time, had been completely omitted by the screenwriter. The *Q.E. II* was carrying a whole party of wealthy American paraplegics in wheelchairs. . . . But this wasn't a Buñuel film.

I may have solved the problems of emotive expression and excessive metaphor—at least provisionally—in the sixties, but that certainly wasn't the case when I began writing *Un Régicide* fifteen years earlier. With a rueful smile I can even point to entire passages in this first attempt at a novel (which wasn't published until much later) that my *A.F.P.* interviewer or the reporter from *L'Express* certainly wouldn't have disowned.

The most obvious of the internal conflicts that structure this narrative is precisely the stylistic tension between fact and expression, that is, between "neutral" writing and the systematic recourse to the pompous attractions of metaphor. In this light the central figure in the text—Boris, the unique, highly personalized narrative consciousness, who even expresses himself in the first person half the time—fits into the illustrious family of the previous decade, exemplified by Camus's Meursault and Sartre's Roquentin.

Doesn't the hero of *L'Etranger* (*The Stranger*) actually

struggle desperately against the world's adjectivity? And isn't it this struggle (perhaps lost in advance) that gives the book its historical importance? In any case, from the opening pages you clearly sense the humanizing metaphors lying in wait for the objective narrative voice, though it's on the lookout—for instance, the famous "drowsy" headland that Sartre in a snap judgment blames on the author's carelessness. It's these metaphors that encroach insidiously every time the dispassionate militance of a well-trained phenomenological technique yields, even momentarily, to sensual pleasure. And of course it's these metaphors, in the long crime scene, that finally break down the last bulwarks of this systematically purified though supposedly natural style, which then seems to be a mask worn by a noble, unhappy soul who was pretending—doubtless for obscure moral reasons—to be nothing but a pure Husserlian consciousness.

As for the philosopher figure in *La Nausée*, he himself admits that it's the aggressive, viscous contingency of the things that make up the external world, the moment you tear away the thin layer of "utility" (or merely of meaning) protecting us and hiding them, that is at once the source of his metaphysical-visceral unease, the object of his passionate fascination, and the initial incentive to keep a diary of "events" (in other words, of his relations with the world) and so produce a narrative. The two scriptural forces engaged here in a fight to the death will be, as we recall, on the one hand the courageous but repellent attempt to capture the events in question, and on the other, the good old conventional attempt to write, in the style of Balzac, the complete, definitive history of the adventurous life of the Marquis de Rollebon (at the same time, alas, enigmatic and full of gaps), a healthy, reassuring, but profoundly dishonest narrative in sympathy with which Sartre/Roquentin also copies out a whole page of *Eugénie Grandet* as an antidote to nausea, in memory of that happy time when it was thought that adjectives were innocent, that reality was clear and precise, and that it could be represented without pitfalls. In any case, the cure doesn't work for long—only a single past historic overflows into the diary's text in the wake of Balzac!

Like these two illustrious godparents (Roquentin and Meursault), Boris has a pervading sense of dislocation, of a division between him and the world—both things and people—that prevents him from really being involved in what's around him, what happens to him, and even his own actions; hence his feeling that he has no reason to exist, that he's superfluous, that he's there by accident, and that no sanction—except social—can ever condemn or vindicate him. His decision to kill the king, less (or more) than a mere sexual impulse of the Oedipal type, at first suggests the ultimate attempt to leap over that gulf, to cross that invisible yet immovable dividing wall, at last to get rid of the diptheritic constriction that even keeps him from breathing. (I think it will now be obvious that I'm deliberately putting the expression of such a desire in sexual terms.)

But regicide is also, of course, the killing of the inscription: inscription of (society's) tables of the law, inscription of death on my tomb. The anagram *ci-gît Red* ("Here lies Red"), which appears shortly after the attack, would accordingly represent the auto-effacement of the capital crime, and consequently the failure (inscribed in advance) of the project of liberation. And so I'm hardly in a position to cast the last stone at the proclaimed failure of Sartre and Camus, unless that stone is also consciously added to my own tumulus.

And I'd like to use all this to return once more to *L'Etranger*, which almost certainly had a profound influence on my literary debut. It's not particularly good form in trendy intellectual circles to acknowledge the influence of Camus's first novel on a whole generation and even beyond. The huge apparatus of symposia and doctoral theses paying tribute to it throughout the world for the last forty years, along with its inordinate public success, immediate and lasting, not to mention the fact that it has been definitively salvaged by all the school textbooks, today makes it almost anathema.

And yet I'm not the only writer—of my age or younger—to place it among the most significant encounters that stand out as milestones in his development. And if I blithely crossed swords with it in the mid-fifties, as I also did with *La Nausée*, it was as much to point out my debt to each of them as to define the direction of my own work by breaking away from both. Besides, every time I reread them (*L'Etranger* in particular, as the text of *La Nausée* has never seemed to me as substantial), they affect me as powerfully as ever.

At the beginning of Camus's narrative, having as yet been only superficially aware of those few drowsy headlands, which we assume (as Sartre did) to be part of the inconsequential flow of an inattentive humanist, we have the startling sensation of having penetrated a consciousness turned exclusively outward, an uncomfortable, highly paradoxical sensation precisely because that consciousness would have no interior, no "inside," affirming its existence at each moment—without continuity—only in so far as (and in the very movement with which) it projects itself constantly outward.

In a short essay written about the same time, it is again Sartre who, to illustrate Husserl's thought, explains to us that if we carelessly entered into such a consciousness we would be unceremoniously cast out, abandoned in the middle of the road in broad daylight, in the world's dry dust, in its blinding light. . . . (I'm quoting from memory, which is totally justified by the willfully subjective nature of my present undertaking.) Do we not recognize here, as if by design, the Algiers setting of our opening pages: the bus ride to the asylum at Marengo, the long walk to the cemetery, the stifling heat on the Mitidja plains scorched by summer? Dry dust and blinding light: this is certainly Meursault's physical-metaphysical universe.

By an astonishing stroke of luck (or genius), Camus will then transform this native landscape, which for him is the place of *familiarity* par excellence, into the very metaphor for *strangeness*, or more accurately, into its "natural" objective correlative. And the book's power comes first of all from this *amazing* presence of the world through the words of a narrator who is outside himself, a tangible world in which we totally, unhesitatingly believe "as if we were there," or better still, so firmly that we can forget its lesson: the sudden, gratuitous appearance of things under the gaze of a blank consciousness strikes us with such crude violence that we hardly notice that it's the perfect, almost didactic representation of the phenomenological experience according to Husserl.

Albert Camus and the sun . . . Albert Camus and Mediterranean beaches. . . . The land where the orange trees of the Goethean soul bloom can't be far away, we think, steeped in Kantian humanism and tranquil happiness. It certainly is the same serene sky, the same inviting sea, the same light, the same heat gently ripening the golden fruit. . . . Not at all! Suddenly everything has changed. It's even as if each of these signs has been inverted: we are poles apart. Certainly Algeria isn't Tuscany, nor even Campania, but above all Goethe, a product of the Nordic mists, had made his Italy into the ideal climate where reason flourished. For him Mediterranean civilization, despite its parched soil and bright light, was the maternal womb, the damp, warm hollow in the shade of the law, the natural cradle of moderation, harmony, eternal wisdom. . . . And now everything here (light, dryness, sun, heat) has become oppressive, extreme, inhuman, charged with menace.

Soon things do in fact deteriorate, while Meursault is revealed as the just opposite of a blank consciousness;

and it's precisely this that is betrayed from the beginning by the few anthropocentric metaphors that escaped his vigilance. He does indeed have an inner consciousness, a full, transcendent interior world in the Kantian mode: hidden within is pure reason, *a priori*, which has always been there since it precedes any lived experience. What this consciousness needed was to feed off the external world, devour it day by day, digest it, and in the end itself become the world, leaving nothing outside.

Through a sort of moral puritanism Meursault claims to refrain in his turn from providing any such social reproduction of ready-made feelings, conventional speech, and codified laws. But it's against his innermost self that he then has to accomplish the inverse movement of digestive appropriation: he has to purge his soul relentlessly by casting himself out, as if he were endlessly bailing out a boat that's taking on water, at the same time unburdening it by throwing overboard the meager treasures stored in its hold.

Now, he does this without realizing that this evacuation (this expulsion) adds day by day to the superfluity outside, while in a parallel action it gradually creates within his unfortunate consciousness a vast empty space maintained at the cost of an increasingly ruinous expenditure of energy, a space that's caving in on all sides. And now we see that this sort of emptiness is merely a parody of a true Husserlian consciousness, which would not have any inside at all and never would have had one; it would be—in the very movement of its projection outward—the simple source of the phenomena that make up the world, whereas Meursault is preparing for a tragic fight to the death against this world.

We soon have an intimation of the inevitable drama: this false stranger will be cornered and will resort to some desperate measure: a cry, an attack, an absurd crime. Or rather, it will happen on its own, outside his control (what a mockery!) for it's the sun, the dry dust, and the blinding light that will commit the crime through his paralyzed hand.

The four brief shots in broad daylight on the deserted, scorching beach blaze out like an anticipated implosion. The dangerous imbalance between the outside world that's too full and this emptied consciousness—not devoid of interiority as it would like to be, but on the contrary, undermined from within by the vacuum it has created—could only explode: in a fraction of a second the soul, completely drained, will reabsorb the whole of the world it rejected, with its adjectives, its emotions, its passions, its madness, and find itself instantly smashed to pieces.

And having imploded, I immediately wake up on the other side of the world in which I've been living until now: I who claimed I could only exist by projecting myself outward, here I am now, by a cruel topological inversion of space, locked in a prison cell, something closed, cubic, probably white, and there's nothing inside these four walls that are now the only outside I'll have, no furniture, no people, no sand, no sea, nothing but me.

What a strange caricature of the maternal womb this sunless hole is, a waiting room for my impending execution, for I am well aware that I will be condemned to death for reasons of implosion. I look out of a small, inaccessible square opening high up in the wall with a new intensity and an emotion that I now accept: I catch every single shade of color in the sky at nightfall, and I "devour with my eyes" every detail of this beautiful clear sky turning imperceptibly pink, mauve, jade green, this time recognizing Latin tranquility: on the other side of my mocking window (the side lost forever), Goethe beckons me once more.

If I'm not contemplating the sky, because it's too dark at night or because of the glare at midday, I try to remember: I attempt a detailed reconstruction of my old room; taking my time, I persist in trying to rediscover all the objects it contained, their exact position and real state, their shape, color, material, as well as tiny flaws or surface damage, accidental, inexplicable—paint flaking off, scratches in the woodwork, small dents in the metal, bumps in the crockery—everything that made them real things and not abstract models. Often, looking for the exact shape of a few millimeters of veneer nicked from the corner of a piece of furniture, for instance, I think I'm maybe making things up, but I see everything so clearly, so distinctly, that I can't tell the difference. And sometimes I even think that what is most real is precisely what I've made up.

Then, when I feel like a rest, I take another look at my press clipping. It's an item from a very old newspaper: doubtless a sexual crime (but for decency's sake the editor couldn't be more explicit), a crime committed against a little girl by a man called Nikolai Stavrogin. Both the reconstruction of the room and the newspaper clipping, which is almost illegible because of the folds in the poor-quality paper, are now in my third novel, *Le Voyeur*. As for the chipped veneer, if I remember rightly, I've already mentioned it in this present work.

But here in my prison cell, where I have all the time in the world to think over these problems, I sometimes suspect I must have confused Henri de Corinthe with the Marquis de Rollebon, to whom I alluded a few pages ago in connection with *La Nausée*, because of certain similarities in their obscure political adventures. This muddle doubtless derives from the mysterious trips that Comte Henri—as my father always called him—made to Russia and Germany toward the end of the thirties or the beginning of the forties, some hundred and fifty years after Rollebon's.

Exactly like Stavrogin in Dostoyevsky's novel, Corinthe is almost always on the move during that frenzied, brutal time. His uncertain activities take place abroad, and we only have fragments that are difficult to piece together, mostly from the accounts (sometimes consistent, sometimes contradictory, in most cases with no obvious connection between them) of third parties who often didn't know him personally. It was obviously in the interest of at least one of these unreliable or frankly suspect witnesses, Alexandre Zara, to lie about his possible relations with other international agitators: we now know for a fact that he himself was a Nazi agent who had worked in London, and that after he was captured by British counterespionage at the end of the war, he always attempted to cover his tracks, not hesitating to compromise innocent people, particularly influential ones.

In September 1938 Corinthe is in Berlin—there seems no doubt about that—and he meets two prominent figures close to the chancellor, one of them several times. But the German newspapers of the period are already presenting him as an invalid who has to spend most of the day resting. Rumors run rife, taken up by the press, about a sword duel in which he was so badly wounded in the throat that the surgeons despaired for his life. The twenty-fourth of that month a reporter visits him at the Astoria Hotel, near Wilhelmstrasse, to interview him about extreme right-wing factions in Europe; he finds himself, he says, in the presence of a much weakened man "wearing a thick white bandage around his neck that could be hiding a brace or even some chance wound or malignant tumor."

However, at the beginning of October (thus, just after the Munich agreements on the Sudetenland), he's in Prague, arriving on the evening of the seventh (by train from Kraków, it's thought), that is, scarcely a few hours before a freight train from Germany blows up, seriously

damaging the famous Wilson Station at the top of Wen-
celas Avenue in the center of the city. The mere presence of such a convoy in a railway station essentially
reserved for passenger travel was already problematic.
The numerous improbabilities in the inconsistent official communiqués the Czech authorities released in the
following days gave rise to the most preposterous sup-
positions. And today, almost half a century later, the
nature of the material in the cars, as well as the technical
cause of the disaster, which seemed to almost everyone to have been a criminal act, is still disputed by historians interested in these preliminaries to the Second
World War.

In any case, Corinthe's presence on the scene hardly
seems coincidental; in a handwritten letter to an unknown recipient, drafted in all probability on the very
day of the catastrophe (it was found after the Allied
victory in the archives of the secret police in Dresden),
Comte Henri gives a detailed inventory of damage
caused to various railway installations, in impersonal
terms that distinctly suggest he's writing a report on a
mission, although it's not possible to determine its exact
nature or for whom it was carried out.

The fact remains that possibly friendly or anyway
cordial relations between Henri de Corinthe and Conrad
Henlein (head of the pro-Nazi party in the Sudetenland
and northern Bohemia) seem to be confirmed by a photograph taken in Paris less than two years earlier, at the
opening of the German pavilion at the 1937 World's
Fair. The two men are perfectly recognizable, laughing
together as they raise their glasses among a group of
German and French notables.

I was fifteen, and I remember with bitterness the
feeling of grotesque disaster throughout France that
day: on the date set for the opening of the fair only two
pavilions were ready, the one for Hitler's Germany and
the one for Soviet Russia, which were curiously alike.

The architecture was massive, square, imposing, decorated with giant statues of a pompous sobriety that today defines the fascist style for us; the two structures stood opposite each other on the right bank of the Seine, by the entrance to the Pont d'Iéna, a huge swastika facing the unfurled hammer and sickle at arm's length. Everything else from the Chaillot hill to the Ecole Militaire was nothing but a vast construction site of rubble and mud—the predictable result of recurrent strikes by of the Popular Front—where a few lost ministers floundered around. The U.S.S.R. and Germany alone had decided to trust only their own workmen and technicians. The comments in my family that evening can well be imagined.

And yet a few weeks later, at the beginning of summer, I remember happy, scorching days and long, delightful strolls through the fairgrounds, finally complete. We went looking for a cool spot under the trees in the unrecognizable landscape that must have been the Champs-de-Mars and the quais; we sought small shady squares between the unlikely, enchanting, astonishing, or simply preposterous constructions, resting a few minutes beside a fountain, drinking exotic fruit juices, nibbling spicy or bittersweet food, before setting off again in search of new discoveries, always with our mother who had a much greater gift for meandering through gardens and pavilions than my father.

Doubtless I was quite ignorant, but I had a vast, dreamy thirst to learn as much as possible, and I was ecstatic about everything. Maman, always approachable, attentive, full of plans (often fanciful), was the ideal companion on these wanderings. For a long time afterward we talked about the inside-out Polish house, the Tunisian *merguez* I tasted for the first time, so delicious that their pungent Oriental scent has remained in my mouth ever since, and then the unknown plants, the Japanese steps, the terraces, and glass walls, or a whole series of louvered Venezuelan shutters in two-tone hardwood, so thin they were translucent. I remember hot nights, too—as if the Parisian climate had also changed for the occasion—and bright lights shining a supernatural green among the chestnut leaves, shedding metallic glittering rays over this imaginary new world.

The importance of things—thin aromatic sausages or electric lights hidden in the foliage—obviously doesn't lie in their intrinsic significance but in the way they stick in our memory. And clearly, the strongest ties between people who are close to each other are above all forged of small, insignificant things. So I'm sure that throughout my childhood and long after I kept alive a dense network of tastes shared with my mother, which probably came from her, but also a solid though more intangible fabric of tiny events and minute sensations that we both experienced in the same way from day to day.

I should mention, for instance, our mutual love of gardens and gardening, a marked gift for culinary invention, our fondness for making complicated, detailed plans in our head (from a simple journey from one place to another in Paris to the complete transformation of a house or neighborhood), a passion for pointless discussions about anything under the sun, preferably irrelevancies, or even, quite simply, our remarkable tendency to waste time doing nothing at all. But all these are still relatively important traits, global options in a way, whereas the most precious things we shared were certainly much more modest, without the slightest universal character, so fragmentary, spontaneous, and transitory that I don't think it's particularly interesting now to search for the best examples. A bluish bird feather, a scrap of foil from a chocolate, a new shoot coming up, a lemon-yellow straw in the dusty road, a red ant carrying a crumb . . . I could take almost any detail at random, since what's essential is how you perceive them and above all how they are woven together.

Papa used to say that my mother and I loved "nooks" (was he using an old-fashioned slang word or a word from the family dialect?). He meant that we were less affected by a vast landscape than by some isolated, unobtrusive, rather marginal element: instead of a great lake viewed from the top of a mountain we preferred the fortuitous arrangement of three mossy stones beside a pool. Sometimes he gently ridiculed Maman's myopia, and also her nose, which he said was gigantic. But I myself had quite normal vision, and I had the same tendency to look at the world from very close up so I could distinguish more and more subtle variations, even when they made no sense.

And probably, like her, I was particularly drawn to objects of a very small size. Throughout my childhood I made myself miniature toys out of the most fragile materials. My parents often told me this story: one year when they asked me what toy I wanted to find on the twenty-fifth of December in front of the black marble fireplace where we excitedly hung up our stockings the night before, I had solemnly asked Father Christmas to bring me "used matchsticks." Our gifts were simple, certainly, but things weren't that bad!

That Christmas they gave me a whole assortment of thin sticks and slats of poplar wood (one or two millimeters thick) as well as a child's set of carpentry tools, just like an adult's: saw, hammer, rasps and files, square, etc., with a selection of nails. Filled with a builder's passion that lasted for months, even years, I

instantly set about constructing miniature houses—
Roman, Etruscan, or Byzantine—inspired by the "*Habitation*" plates in the two-volume *Larousse.*

I also spent whole days classifying things, putting
them in small cardboard boxes, labeling them as carefully as if they were in a museum display case laid out
neatly on beds of cotton wool: the mouth parts of lob-
sters and sea urchins dismantled and painstakingly
cleaned, and other collections of worthless stuff, thorns
from different bushes, beetles with iridescent metallic
elytra, fossil nummulites split in two along the circum-
ference to show the spiral chamber where the protozoa
once lived, fragile, diaphanous shells with rose-petal
whorls, picked up on the beach, dried, and chosen for
their delicate pearly colors.

Yes, okay, I'm coming to it: I also had two china dolls
a few centimeters high, which I used to dress and un-
dress. They were obviously not baby dolls but already
little girls. Doubtless I was faithful to them for a very
long time, since they—bound hand and foot, naturally—were the the beneficiaries of my first erotic practices. In fact, my perverse tastes were so precocious that
when I think about it they must have preceded any
heterosexual consciousness: I cheerfully dreamed of the
massacre of my classmates (and the primary schools
weren't coed), but the ones I considered ugly or didn't
like were summarily disposed of, simply to get rid of
them, whereas the graceful bodies with pretty, delicate
faces enjoyed long-drawn-out torture sessions tied to
the chestnut trees in the playground.

Meticulous, sadistic, and thrifty as well, I here admit
in front of good old Doctor Freud that from the earliest
age I combined these three attributes from which he
created one of his favorite complexes. And for the bene-
fit of his present or future descendants I'd also like to
point out to all and sundry that I sucked at the maternal
breast until I was over two years old, and since I was
already walking and talking almost fluently, I could

demand this exclusive nourishment in clear terms, with a phrase that has remained legendary in the family: "Not cup milk, Mommy's milk."

Maman was always meticulous and patient, even when performing the most trivial tasks, and also had a knack for turning most of them into games. As for her love of very small things, it was so well known in the family and among friends that everyone liked to bring her little gifts from their travels. There's still a glass case at Kerangoff with miscellaneous objects on display, from Cévenol kitchen utensils just a few millimeters in size to Japanese figurines made from grains of rice.

But any issue of an explicitly carnal nature, or even implicitly erotic, radically separated us. Very early on I'd sensed that there was no possible meeting ground on that subject. And I, who told her everything, was instinctively silent about my cruel imaginary scenes and nocturnal pleasures. Whenever anyone mentioned sexual complications of any kind—apart from lesbian relations (sentimental or otherwise, I don't know), which she always seemed to treat indulgently—these were (at least in conversation) smilingly denounced as more degrading than anything else, and maybe that went for so-called normal coition too.

Nevertheless, I am convinced that she had no trace of puritanism or prudery. Her relations with the world were openly sensual, leaving no room for hypocritical disguise. Besides, she talked about everything very freely for the time, laughing, for instance, at the sodomist propaganda one of her friends from the past apparently went in for, or giving a young girl this kind of advice: "There are boys you sleep with but don't marry"—a verdict delivered with the same authority she assumed in judging people categorically and definitively on first meeting.

Today I tell myself that she must have felt a much greater complicity when it came to female pleasure; she was always more or less accusing male sexual pleasure of being violent, simplistic, and crude. After reading *La Nausée* because of my interest in the book, she pronounced an irrevocable judgment on Roquentin because he asked his girlfriend (I've never checked this in the text) for oral favors. She always had such immediate and passionate contact with everything, real or imaginary, that the hero of a novel—albeit the messenger of a new metaphysic—seemed first and foremost someone with whom she did or didn't wish to associate. In effect my mother was saying to me: Your friend Roquentin is a repulsive creep, don't bother to invite him here again! She was very excitable. I would answer with a smile, "You're overdoing it a bit!" But quite soon I gave up trying to make her share my way of reading literature.

And yet, could my judgment be clouded by a sense of personal guilt influencing my impressions of her reaction to this disturbing realm of eros? In any case, her attitude toward men and their fantasies seemed all the more striking in that she showed a kind of protective universal tenderness toward the mating of animals, birds or cats, even certain tomcats that manifested their strongly sadoerotic tendencies in front of her. As with all my manuscripts when I began writing, my mother was the first to read *Le Voyeur*. When she'd finished, she said to me, "I think it's a remarkable book, but I would have preferred that it had not been written by my son"—as I've already mentioned.

At an international conference a few years ago I heard a well-known director—Indian or Egyptian, I forget— explain to an audience of spellbound film buffs that his main concern when shooting a scene could be summed up by the simple question: Will my mother understand, will she like what I'm doing? Telling stories to your mother, both audience and supreme judge—after all, why not? It's as good a criterion as any. But I probably didn't write my novels for mine, nor produce my films to please her. Would that mean I was working against her? I don't think so, although my apparent predilection for dispassionate narrative may be seen as a sort of defensive reaction against the too fervent subjectivity with which she expressed her feelings.

And yet if you took that point of view, you could just as well say that I started to write (and then make films) in that objective way out of a distrust of my own inclinations or even in open conflict with myself. For I did share with my mother the questionable taste for a whole literature of passion and despair—as described earlier—whereas my father would furiously interrupt her over-impassioned reading of *Jude the Obscure*, leaping up and throwing the book on the floor, and could hardly be restrained from trampling it underfoot in a healthy reaction of self-defense. As for me, I cried my eyes out over the harrowing ending of *Crossroads*, and it was no consolation when they tried to pacify me by saying that it wasn't a true story, that the author had made it all up on purpose to catch me in his trap.

So even if I do work against many of my inclinations, it's for myself alone that I write and make films, and I have to laugh when an erudite film critic explains to his countless fans in yet another article condemning me that Robbe-Grillet, alas, still hasn't understood the specifically "popular" nature of the seventh art (which would then be no art at all, since art can only be personal). And with this book too, which seems to be meant for the reader or even the critic, I'm not at all sure that I'm not, as usual, the unique target. You always create for yourself, even if you do dream of worldwide sales or packed houses.

Unconsciously I might have made up stories to control my increasingly compulsive criminal fantasies (the ghost of the Marquis de Sade coming to pull me out of bed), but at the same time, on the contrary, in order to conquer the excessive sensitivity of a tenderhearted, backward crybaby who could grieve for days over negligible, often imaginary heartbreaks, dwelling on them until a lump formed in his throat and his eyes filled with tears—especially if they had to do with very young women or little children. An example suddenly comes to mind, hidden away for at least half a century . . .

Our father is scarcely more than five or six years old. This is in the Haut-Jura. His gang of friends, boys and girls, has decided to make a cake, and each one has to bring some utensil or ingredient. My dear father in his school smock goes off happily to meet the others, carefully holding the precious lump of butter that his mother has given him for this important occasion. But once they're together again, the novice pastry chefs quarrel. They won't make anything after all. And the little child returns all alone, toddling along in the sun on the same winding path between the meadows, stumbling blindly, sniffling, desperately disappointed, his heart suddenly bursting with all the misery in the world, the clumsily rewrapped, useless lump of butter gradually melting in his hands. Why did he tell us about this trivial mishap? Why was he so excessively distressed that he still remembers the whole episode forty years later?

Naturally it's Catherine who moves me most easily to pity, vain tenderness, and foolish indulgence now, since she's my wife and my children too, and I feel totally responsible for her, for her happiness, though she gets along very well on her own; I feel guilty if she suffers, even if it has nothing to do with me. And so our life together seems to be strewn with small, sad stories where I suddenly find myself completely at a loss again, clumsy, beside myself in the face of inconsolable, heartrending fits of despair that will still scar my memory when Catherine has long forgotten them.

For example: Soon after our marriage, we are living on Boulevard Maillot in the new apartment we owe to Paulhan's discreet kindness. I've been taking an afternoon nap, as I often do since my "colonial" stint a long time ago, while my child wife has gone to pick up some net curtains from the cleaners. When I emerge from my room, I see her stricken face and meet eyes swollen with barely suppressed tears. In response to my anxious questions, unable to contain herself any longer, she bursts into painful, harrowing sobs; spasms of grief contort her features, and she can hardly manage to murmur the irrevocable: "My curtain, they've torn it."

A banal laundry accident, sure, but at the sight of the hideous, jagged tear in the almost new muslin, I share her misery with all my soul. And then, above all, this is Catherine and I love her and that's no help to her at all, and she looks like a little waif abandoned in the ruins. . . . It's the period when it seems hard to believe that she's no longer a child but really a young woman. When she took her wedding dress to be cleaned before the ceremony (a private civil ceremony, don't worry) because the dressmaker had delivered it slightly soiled, the same cleaner (who didn't know her then) took pains to explain to her, as if to a child who might not understand, "Next time, dear, you must tell your mommy to unstitch the lining first." "Yes, madame," Catherine answered without missing a beat.

Faced with a salesman who rings the bell and asks disconcerted by her size and appearance, if there's anyone home, she simply says, "No, no one," almost believing it herself, and shuts the door, locking it for safety. In Hamburg two years later, after a lecture I've just given at the French Institute, our consul general decides to say something nice to this pretty young girl lost among all the grown-ups: "Don't you get bored, mademoiselle, accompanying your daddy on lecture tours?" But this time she replies with her most winning smile, "He's not my daddy, monsieur, he's my husband!" The poor diplomat doesn't know what to do with himself, while she and I, accomplices, are delighted by his mistake.

Actually, age hasn't got anything to do with it, nor has face or character. After so many years together setting up house or traveling the world, despite her independent life, her many close friends, and her happy self-sufficiency, Catherine is still my little girl. And so I'll end this insistent sentimental passage with a very recent scene.

I've been alone at Le Mesnil for several days; I'm waiting impatiently for her to come back that evening, as arranged. She arrives at last, very late at night, as usual. I don't know what to do to celebrate her return, despite her obvious irritation when I confess my irrational anxiety; when I wait like that all evening at a window on the first floor, watching for her headlights through the trees at the entrance to the grounds, I invariably imagine that she's lost, that goodness knows what has happened to her, just as Maman used to do when I came home later than the time she'd set or reckoned I'd be back.

And then because I'm clumsy opening a cupboard or because things are in an awkward place through bad luck, I knock a lamp made from a transparent glass demijohn off the corner of the cherrywood sideboard in the kitchen. The fragile sphere smashes to smithereens on the flagstones. Catherine cries out like a wounded bird, her voice incredulous, beseeching: "Oh! No!" In the ensuing silence she stands quite still for a moment contemplating the disaster at her feet; then she leans down slowly and gently picks up some of the larger sharp splinters, slender as a dream, as if there were still hope of sticking them together again. But soon, discouraged, she drops them back on the floor and murmurs in a subdued voice as desolate as lost happiness, "It was like a big blue bubble . . ."

It wasn't a very valuable object, only an old hand-blown bottle from the past that she'd found in the cellar, miraculously intact without its protective basket, when she was sorting out the house in Bourg-la-Reine after her grandmother's death. But I knew she was very fond of it—as a souvenir of her childhood, maybe—because of its extremely delicate glass and very pale bluish color, whereas most old demijohns are greenish and much coarser.

There you are. Irreparable. I hug Catherine with all my strength, trying to console her. I know very well I can't help. In the night that now tastes of ashes, I reverently place the remains of the demijohn in the mortuary hollow of a cardboard box, as a token (I say as an excuse) of the hope—who knows?—of one day finding another just like it in some country junk shop. But to this day I still haven't found anything.

I've often been asked why there's so much broken glass in my films, from *Marienbad* to *La Belle Captive* (and long before the accident I've mentioned here). I usually answer that it makes an interesting noise (an ensemble of crystalline sounds across a broad spectrum, which enables Michel Fano to introduce various transformations with the help of a synthesizer), and also that the scattered fragments catch the light so prettily . . .

But I'm perfectly aware that this kind of explanation is never satisfactory. On the other hand, I don't see any affective relation between the sound images I've been able to produce with such material, constantly orchestrated in new combinations, and this bitter episode in the family history (which happened much later, I repeat). Nevertheless, there *must* be a connection. And now the link has been made structurally anyway: through the rapprochement that's just taken place as I write.

145

As for the desperate feelings of paternal love—incestuous, needless to say—that Catherine inspired in me from our first meeting, my mother was surprised (doubtless alarmed) that they could coincide with the writing of *Le Voyeur*, in which a precocious little girl played quite a different role. But in this case, on the contrary, the connection is obvious. For from my point of view this novel that she found so shocking remains in spite of everything loving, limitless, extravagant.

Le Voyeur was published in the spring of 1955, also by Editions de Minuit, with substantial extracts running at the same time in two successive issues of *La Nouvelle N.R.F.*, which had just appeared. Unlike *Les Gommes*, which had passed virtually unnoticed two years before, only attracting the attention of a few rummagers such as Barthes or Cayrol, the new book benefited from a small scandal the moment it appeared, with staunch supporters and passionate detractors hurling insults—just what it takes in Paris to make a name in the republic of letters. I owed this sudden spotlight mostly to Georges Bataille and the Prix des Critiques, an important award at the time because of the prestigious jury and the recent winners: Camus and Sagan.

The prize was awarded in May at a meeting of literary experts where violent enmity seemed the rule. Bataille, Blanchot, Paulhan, etc., were on my side, and against me were all the influential Academy critics who wrote for the daily papers and literary periodicals—the "ground floor," it was said, because their articles took up the whole bottom third of the page. After the modernists won a narrow victory in a battle that raged for several hours, the furious losers instantly gave me the best publicity a writer could possibly dream of: Henri Clouard resigned from the jury in a huff, while the gentle Emile Henriot demanded in *Le Monde* that I be committed to a lunatic asylum or brought up on a misdemeanor, if not a felony!

All this uproar, plus the enthusiastic praise of Roland Barthes in *Critique* and Maurice Blanchot in *N.R.F.* (tributes that were incompatible, by the way, Blanchot seeing only the sexual crime and Barthes blithely ignoring it), obviously gained me a few readers and a budding notoriety. Albert Camus and André Breton gave me warm encouragement. *L'Express* opened its columns to me for a series of articles on "literature today," which were the origin of the "manifestos" subsequently published in *N.R.F.* and later of the essay *Pour un nouveau roman (For a New Novel)*.

And this is also the moment when Dominique Aury finds it imperative to lose the rejection letter I received from Gaston Gallimard a few years earlier for *Un Régicide*. It was a short typewritten note on a small piece of letterhead. Although I'm not sure of the exact wording, I remember its contents perfectly. The rough meaning was: Your story is interesting, but as it doesn't appeal to any kind of public, we feel it's pointless to publish it. A few mimeographed copies would be sufficient for its circulation. However, Jean Paulhan, who's always liked eccentrics, has taken note of it and will get in touch with you should the occasion arise . . .

When Paulhan's precious assistant asks me to lend her this document on the pretext of finding out who wrote it, it doesn't occur to me that they must have a copy on file in Rue Sébastien-Bottin. So I hand over the original without making a photocopy, which wasn't normally done at the time anyway. And when I ask for my letter back a few months later, Dominique Aury is thunderstruck: What letter? Gallimard can't have rejected *Un Régicide* since they never had it under consideration! Isn't that so, Jean? —Really, Dominique, you remember: I gave you the manuscript personally when you were living at the Cité Universitaire. —Oh, yes, I remember; but I passed it on to Editions Robert Whatshisname, and they immediately agreed to publish it . . . sadly, just before they went bankrupt. Etc.

I say no more. I'm stunned—it's all a bit much. Paulhan flashes his legendary smile at me, radiating innocent candor, amused, benevolent, charming, and inscrutable: impossible to say whether this is the genuine surprise of an old man who has very conveniently forgotten all about it, or the jubilation of a kid who's just pulled off a successful trick. Nathalie Sarraute used to say: He's Talleyrand, and Dominique Aury is Fouché! And yet I was fond of them both and admired Paulhan, the man as well as his work, and still do. I also appreciated the inimitable way in which he, who never hesitated to help his protégés, would suddenly make them ill at ease (for example, by systematically praising such and such a detail in one of my books . . . when it didn't exist). As for Dominique Aury, it was she—and this she willingly admits—who turned *Un Régicide* over to Georges Lambrichs after Gallimard rejected it, while I was looking after my banana trees in the Antilles. In a way, it was she who introduced me to Editions de Minuit, and I'm very grateful to her. Besides, this vanishing trick with a letter thought to be compromising was actually rather flattering to me.

It was also that summer that I met Bruce Morrissette, an American university expert on fake Rimbauds, who'd come to Paris from Saint Louis, Missouri, for the publication of a huge scholarly tome titled *La Chasse Spirituelle* (an astute analysis that managed to cause a misunderstanding between him and André Breton, as well as Maurice Nadeau and everyone whose name was rashly mixed up in this amusing affair). Morrissette, having heard about my book on the radio by chance, wanted to meet me. We immediately became friends. Intelligent, highly cultured, excited by all forms of modernism (I think it was he who first told me about Robert Rauschenberg, best known in his early years for erasing a very beautiful pencil drawing by his elder, De Kooning—as a pictorial gesture), he also had a sense of humor, rather a rare find among professors of literature; he felt that works of art are made for fun, that they are the "Sunday of life" announced by Hegel.

Two or three years later, when Morrissette was back in France, he asked to be invited to Brest, to the maternal home at Kerangoff, which I had talked to him about. The whole family welcomed him with open arms, as is their way, my mother offering her unfailing hospitality to distant relatives and passing strangers with an old-fashioned liberality that I unfortunately haven't inherited from her. For my part, I made every effort to take my American friend around and show him what I thought had motivated his visit: the cliffs, dunes, heaths, and sandy beaches among the rocks that had influenced my Breton childhood and were transposed as the setting for *Le Voyeur*. But apart from the megalithic monuments we came across on our travels, he scarcely seemed interested in the landscape of Léon.

On the other hand, at home he enthusiastically talked with my mother about everything under the sun. I thought he was merely being polite. After a few days he told me he was going to leave, assuring me that his stay had been very productive: he'd found what he was looking for. I asked him what that was. Bruce Morrissette answered me very simply: before devoting himself entirely to my work, he wanted to be sure that I was a genuinely great writer; now, geniuses necessarily have exceptional mothers; and now he knew that mine was! I must add that it was quite courageous of him to gamble on the work of a novelist who was just starting out, as it was only in the sixties—and doubtless partly thanks to him—that I become a star topic in universities on the other side of the Atlantic.

Was our sainted mother—as we often called her—"exceptional"? Of course at home this formed part of the family credo. But we all tended to think we were all exceptional. Besides, who isn't the minute you look at them more closely? It's in the acute consciousness of such individuality that the clan spirit originates. However, it must be said that Maman generally made a very strong impression on those who met her. The daughter of the Olgiatti woman (whom I've already mentioned with regard to our education) called my mother "godmother," although there was no reason to, since she had neither been baptized nor been given the first name Yvonne, and she used to repeat admiringly, "You're as*ton*ishing!" This apostrophe, with the heavy local accent on the central syllable, remained part of our folklore.

This lore was very rich and consisted of all kinds of stories drawn from daily life but progressively distorted by legend until they were unrecognizable. So my mother, it was said, long before the 1914 war and ever since, had insisted on fixing up the back of the small grocery shop in Rue de la Porte at Recouvrance, which her mother had managed in the first years of this century or right at the end of the last, while Grandfather Canu was on active service. The grocery and the house it was in had disappeared long ago, destroyed by bombs in 1945, and the old Rue de la Porte vanished when the bulldozers leveled and straightened poor Brest after the Second World War. But it would take more than that to stop our mythical mother from solving certain subtle problems of partitions and inconvenient passageways.

There was also the famous "bus scene." In a traffic jam near Printemps our mother allegedly pushed my sister and me in front of a bus as it was moving off. As her children shrank back terrified, she apparently ridiculed such a vulgar instinct for self-preservation, declaring in a loud voice, "It's better to die young." Another time, in the only room of a Spartan inn in the Arrée Mountains, where all four of us were staying on one of our walking tours across the Brittany interior (*ar coat* in Breton), I had a violent attack of indigestion in the middle of the night. Our mother, all a-tremble, deciding that the husband she'd rudely awakened was taking too long to light a candle, leapt at him brandishing a large knife, ready to strike him! This episode was referred to as "Brasparts' knife" (thus immortalizing the name of the place), and Papa used to recount it solemnly in tragic Racinian accents to anyone who'd listen, turning his wife into "the bloody Athalie."

The chronicle also contained less extravagant tales, more likely if not more truthful, in particular concerning my mother's incredible faculty for forgetting the time, that is, for losing time (though I'm certainly not the one to reproach her), which meant that she might arrive anywhere at any hour and with perfect equanimity serve meals when everyone else had gone to bed or the guests had long since left on an empty stomach to catch the last metro. My grandmother would say to her, "My poor child, you're on the road to ruin!" And I can certainly guarantee the authenticity of the ritual "watercress soup" phenomenon, which took place at regular intervals.

When it was already very late in the evening, Maman would begin preparing dinner, washing a bunch of watercress her husband had picked up after work. Soon she would notice that the stems tied with string or raffia hid a mass of aquatic insects, mollusks, worms, or freshwater crustaceans, such as water scorpions, backswimmers, tiny leeches, lymnaeids, or planorbids. There were lots of gammarids, a kind of minute amphipod shrimp that we wrongly called daphnids and were particularly fond of because of the way they wiggled as they swam. Maman would immediately begin to gather up all the little creatures that were still alive and put them into a jar with a few pieces of cress for company, making a miniature aquarium that I spent hours gazing at in wonder. Papa had had his coffee, garlic sausage, and bread long ago; he would go off to bed with an exaggerated downcast air ("Comedian!" my mother would say to him) and in the stricken tones of a prophet preaching to deaf ears he would utter this saying—I don't know where it came from—"And tomorrow they'll all be dead at Picard's!" And the children, who were dawdling over their homework—French composition or Latin translation—wouldn't have their soup till one or two in the morning and would have trouble getting up for school. As for Maman, she would spend the rest of the night reading her papers.

Her almost obsessive concern for all forms of animal life was certainly one of the dominant traits in her character, and anecdotes abound. There was the story of the tench my father brought home alive for a special lunch: they were instantly plunged into a bucket of fresh water and fed for several months until the summer vacation when we set them free in the pond in Montsouris Park the day before we left, hiding from groundskeepers who would have thought that on the contrary we were trying to catch them. The nice fish were so used to their gilded metal home that Maman, who wouldn't have dreamed of harming them by firmly dumping them out, had the greatest trouble coaxing them to leave the largely submerged bucket on their own.

I've already described the famous jackdaw that had fallen out of some nest in Paris and was raised at liberty in the small apartment, where it destroyed a great deal of wallpaper by tearing off the loose bits, until it was taken to Kerangoff, and lived there for many years, half wild, half tame. Back in Paris, Maman nursed a young swift weakened by the frightful parasites in its feathers, giving it a horse tonic for convalescents. After the bird was cured, it often came to visit us through the "study" window, which we left open on purpose. On the narrow balcony we had tubs containing our two miniature gardens—one called "the Sahara," the other "the Jura"—which took a lot of looking after: tidying the ragged contours, replanting, cutting back overgrown vegetation, raking the sandy paths, etc. In the ten square centimeters of lake there were watercress fauna, of course, as well as tiny newts whose feeding habits, couplings, and moltings kept us occupied for entire afternoons.

Sadly, a sick bat eventually died after weeks of care. It was a tiny vespertilio whose corpse weighed less than three grams. Too weak to hibernate, suffering from a vitamin deficiency, it lived under Maman's blouse (in what she called her pouch) next to her warm body—to the great terror of uninitiated visitors who thought they were hallucinating when they looked at their impassive hostess whose tea they were politely sipping, and saw the creature suddenly emerge from its hiding place through the narrow opening of a white collar with large lapels, to clamber awkwardly over her breast and neck spreading its huge, black, silky wings.

Another, much more personal memory from further back in the past now rises out of the darkness like a bad dream. I'm very small, very nervous, very alone, lost in huge empty corridors with very high ceilings. At last going through the imposing glass door of the building where our classrooms are, I come out into the fresh air and sunlight of the deserted playground, where the tall, stout, gnarled trunks of the chestnut trees (them again) stand in rows like blackish pillars. It must be toward the end of my first year in primary school in Rue Boulard, where I am pampered by a nice smiling teacher with the transparent name of Monsieur Clair. I still have my long curly hair and my girlish look. Seized by an urgent need,

I've had to ask permission to leave class. It's already late spring, as the chestnut's new leaves are very thick and green.

Just where the sunlight and the shadow cast by the first tree meet on the gravel, there's a fallen sparrow fledgling that can't fly or stand up. Half paralyzed, I hold my breath as I come down the three long steps leading to the playground. The bird must be injured, or it wouldn't be dragging itself around in circles like this. My mother would have picked it up instantly, examined it, looked after it, disinfected its wounds, put a splint on its broken wing. . . . Away from her, I don't know what to do for this fragile ball of feathers struggling and cheeping softly.

Overcome by a sudden impulse to put an end to its suffering, I put my foot on it and press. This is not just a snail. It's much firmer and more resistant. And I'm also afraid of causing pain as I crush this thing that's still alive. Panic-stricken, I end up using all my childish strength. It squishes under my shoe. I feel I've committed a sordid murder. Soon I realize, terrified, that there's blood on my sole and even a bit of gray down stuck to it, which I can't get off as I scrape my feet on the gravel and run, weak at the knees, heart thumping, to the row of toilets at the end of the playground, where the half doors will only provide a temporary barrier against the overwhelming horror I feel.

That day I can't think of anything else—as if my shoe kept crushing the tiny bird's body over and over again—until school's over and I rush to Maman, who's waiting for me at the school gates, to tell her in floods of tears about my incomprehensible crime. Last month, near the landing at the lower pond at Le Mesnil, I deliberately crushed a baby nutria under my boot (I think its proper name is muskrat or ondatra). These big aquatic and terrestrial rodents are to be found in profusion in Normandy since the war, when much of the local breeding stock was loosed into the wild during the fighting, so they say, and Catherine worries when they multiply along the river, because they weaken the banks and bring down the trees among whose roots they've built their labyrinthine galleries. I had the same terrible feeling I'd had before, and thought that the poor squashed sparrow must be a real memory and not, as is so often the case, a story my parents told me later.

Of course our mother taught us to read, write, and count, and to speak properly. So the early grades were easy for us. Besides, although dreamy and reflective by temperament—a form of laziness—I've always enjoyed learning. This is doubtless part of a vast longing to possess the world (to *have* in order to *be*), just like collecting stamps, plants, or miscellaneous objects, like the obsession with ordering everything, the impossibility of throwing anything away, the habit of taking hundreds of slides (later to be classified and arranged in boxes) in every new country I visit, or of learning by heart great chunks of beloved poetry or prose. It is a common illusion: the instinct to hoard (knowledge or anything else) is part of the will to power, which is to say, the instinct for self-preservation. Only later, much later, do you realize that the things you've accumulated are ranged on the side of death.

But the absolute value of knowledge for its own sake, in all fields, has always been one of the keystones of the family ideology inherited from the grandfathers—teachers or coastguards, right wing or left. Grandmother Canu ran a grocery store (which she didn't own) in a poor neighborhood, but she had her diploma.

Today I still have this appetite for learning, above all if it involves an exercise of intellect or memory. And I find that one of the attractions of the university professor's life, which I lead from time to time in America (in New York or on some lost campus in one of those enormous states with legendary names), is that I instantly become a student again. Serious pupils (mine are usually "graduate students"), theoretical discussions with the other teachers, peaceful settings, the cozy atmosphere of a cultural ghetto, of extraterritoriality (out of my country, out of time)—all this gives me back the eager, ambitious, and gratuitous freedom of adolescence, when there's still a whole lifetime of learning ahead. I discover, I fill in the gaps, I reread closely, taking notes, I go to the library for one or another of those heavy seminal works I've always put off reading for lack of time or energy.

I also try to restore a faith in culture in those of my students who have lost it, I rehabilitate intellectual pleasure, the primacy of the mind, and even—why not?—elitist pride. In the old days, in our simple home, we weren't ashamed to say, "*Odi profanum vulgus et arceo.*" And I passionately condemn the mindless evenings in front of the "tube" and the sheeplike consumption of the latest pulp best-seller, as well as the costly tripe launched by the huge mass-media circus of the California film industry, where the least gag weighs a ton, not to mention what they do to disciplines that are pretty heavy to begin with, such as psychoanalysis, Boy Scout ethics, and social realism.

But I have to be careful over there too. If I say outright that most of Hitchcock's or Minnelli's films are simply standard, more or less well-made products, I will doubtless be accused either of my known taste for provocation or of resenting their worldwide success both in the press and with the public.

So I was a gifted pupil and enjoyed studying, but—hereditary taint or infectious illness caught in the cradle—I was also perpetually behind with my work (things haven't changed much since), so much so that a bad conscience has always been my daily lot. At four-thirty in the morning, when we heard the musical clanging racket of the milkman unloading his heavy metal cans at the dairy across the street, then piling the empties onto the big open wagon drawn by two Percherons, my sister and I were often still working by lamplight on either side of the double desk—the arrival of the milk representing, however, a fateful deadline that couldn't be ignored, even if the French composition or the Greek translation wasn't finished.

Homework turned in late, lessons learned at the last minute (on the way to school) or entrusted to the grace of God (brushing a finger along the tree trunks from one end of the boulevard to the other without stepping on the iron grills was a powerful charm against being questioned in class, while you only needed one tree—preferably with smooth bark—if you put your whole hand on it and said a magic spell, one I still use from time to time to calm all sorts of fears), exercise books copied out neatly in an impeccable manner but never on time and increasingly out of phase with the calendar as the school year went on—all this meant that the results weren't always praised by the teachers.

When they were plainly mediocre, my father would instantly talk of getting us an apprenticeship, since we weren't up to this needlessly costly secondary education. My mother would plead our cause and convince him to give us another chance for one more year. In the end both of us came through and finished the course that was considered the most prestigious at the time—Latin, Greek, mathematics—and with fairly good grades at that.

I won a state scholarship in a reputedly difficult competitive exam and got into the Lycée Buffon as a day boarder after a memorable scene. As usual my hair was too long. Having drawn my mother's attention to this fact at the last minute, while she's in a flap about the time because she's got to come with me to the principal's office for my official introduction, I hear myself saying that it won't show because I'll wear my hat (a sort of silky felt bowler that accentuates my round cheeks and dainty appearance). Good. I assume it's settled. So there we both are, formally seated opposite the florid, bald headmaster, who's had his piggy little eyes fixed on me ever since we came in, while Maman tries to distract him from her late arrival and knocks herself out extolling the virtues of her offspring.

"Well now, here's a little boy who must be very proud of his headgear, which is doubtless why he keeps it glued to his head like that," the fat man with the glistening pink skin finally pronounces from behind his august desk, having taken all that time to polish his subtle reference (I imagine) to Charles Bovary's first day at school. My mother, scandalized by my bad manners, which she's just now noticed, tears the offending object from my head, and the mass of carefully hidden curls comes tumbling down. . . . We argued for years afterward about whether she had or hadn't told me to keep my hat on in front of the headmaster.

And then—possibly the next year—comes a much more disturbing incident in which this same character plays an ambivalent role, while a tall senior master with a very black square beard takes the part of the methodical sadopedophile after the mysterious business of the schoolbags swapped during gym class, administering sharp blows with a ruler to our naked calves during private sessions in his den that he called "flogging number one, two, or three" according to the severity of the penalty. This repeated punishment for an imaginary crime whose exact nature was never explained to me, and which seems to be the pure stuff of nightmares (sexual?), upset me for months because it was so absurd: complete absence of facts, plausibility, cause and effect, logical organization of predicates—in a word, of "realism." Again it was my mother, alarmed by the red weals on the back of my legs, who went to the administrative authorities to try and clear up the mystery—the whole thing—to me at least—remained utterly obscure.

On the other hand, it was my father who came to my defense several grades later when I was expelled as a day boarder "for saying *shit* to a teaching assistant." In fact I hadn't addressed him at all but only muttered to myself a little too loudly, "Shit, you can't even do your work here anymore!" after the irritable teacher had forbidden me to go to my box at the back of the classroom to get my Latin dictionary. Papa, his anarchist-libertarian spirit rekindled, had pounced on the stupefied headmaster and announced in no uncertain terms that he thought he'd sent his son to a lycée, not to the Jesuits or a school for the Children of Mary.

And so I continued at school as a day student, which meant without teaching assistants or use of the canteen; but we had a bit more money at home then, and Lina, the formidable Swiss housekeeper, made me infinitely superior meals. My father still took us to school every morning, our respective "institutions" being quite near each other. He strode along, his two children trotting by his side, down Avenue du Maine, Boulevard de Vaugirard, and Boulevard Pasteur. From the top of Boulevard Pasteur, outlined against the sky above the trees, the turreted roofs of the main school building suddenly appeared, slates shining in the morning sun, intricate as a Renaissance château—which was why we baptized my lycée "Schloss-Buffon" in honor of Chamisso de Boncour, whose moving poem to the lost Fatherland we declaimed in German as we went down the middle of the boulevard.

All this is real, that is to say, fragmentary, fleeting, useless, so accidental and so specific that any incident at any moment appears gratuitous and any life seems in the end devoid of the slightest unifying signification.

The advent of the modern novel is precisely linked to this discovery: reality is discontinuous, composed of elements juxtaposed at random, each of them unique and all the more difficult to grasp in that they emerge in an always unforeseen, irrelevant, haphazard way.

Anglo-Saxon essayists trace the birth of the novel as a genre back to the beginning of the eighteenth century—not before—when Defoe, then Richardson and Fielding decide that reality exists in the here and now, not elsewhere in some "better" timeless otherworld characterized by coherence. Henceforth the real world will no longer be located in an abstract (perfect) idea of things, of which everyday life is at best merely a pale reflection, but will be found in the things themselves, here on earth, as each person sees them, hears them, touches them, feels them, according to his lived experience.

In consequence reality, which hitherto lay exclusively in the general and the universal (the famous Scholastic "universals"), is suddenly revealed to be so particular that it becomes impossible to slot it into categories of meaning, save at the cost of serious reductive distortions. What from then on will be called *novel*, to emphasize the novelty of the genre, will stick exclusively to concrete (which doesn't mean objective) details, fragments related with meticulous simplicity, even if this should undermine (and certainly it soon does) the possibility of constructing an image of unity, or of any totality whatsoever.

Thus the coherence of the world begins to collapse. And yet the narrator's authority at first seems to remain unassailable; you could almost say that he has more authority, since there's no longer any other world to describe but the very one he knows. We've come down to earth, but more than ever it's a kind of man-god who's speaking. Now he simply attaches himself to small immediate things rather than lofty mediatized concepts.

Not until Laurence Sterne and Diderot will the narrative voice claim both its total creative freedom and its sweeping lack of authority, affirming with a smile of complicity at each twist and turn of the text: No one knows what all this means, I no more than you, and besides, what does it matter, since I can invent anything at all? We recall the startling opening of *Jacques le fataliste* (*Jacques the Fatalist*) and are reminded of the beginning of *L'Innommable* (*The Unnameable*), written by Samuel Beckett nearly two centuries later.

But after that exhilarating prerevolutionary period, when the notion of truth (divine as well as human) is blithely called into question, after the chaos of bloody revolutions, regicides, and so-called wars of liberation, we have the inevitable backlash: when all is said and done, it's the bourgeoisie—monarchist and Catholic—that takes power in France. And the new values that they venerate demand, on the contrary, absolutely fixed meanings, the seamless plenitude of reality, chronological and causal guarantees, noncontradiction with no possible deviation. This is a far cry from Jacques's wanderings, with their unexpected spatial dislocations, their parodoxical episodic adventures, and their casual bifurcations or inversions of time—certainly much farther than Jacques is from us today. With Balzac the coherence of the world and the narrator's authority are both pushed to a limit that has never been reached since.

The "realist" ideology is born: the world, closed and complete in a definitive, weighty, unequivocal rigidity, is entirely permeable to meaning, novelistic elements are classified and put into a hierarchy, the linear plot unfolds according to the reassuring laws of reason, and the characters become types—the miserly old man, the ambitious young man, the devoted mother, etc. The universal returns at full gallop.

And even when Balzac denounces the fragmentation of human labor, and the resulting fragmentation of the whole of society and of individual consciousness (which leads the Marxist Lukács to consider him a revolutionary writer struggling against capitalist industrialization and the alienation it produces), he does so from the heart of a text in which on the contrary everything reassures the triumphant bourgeoisie: for the reader, the innocent, serene continuity of the narration dispels any fear of a serious (structural) flaw in the system. The undisturbed exercise of power and the annexation of the world by one class are just and necessary, since the great novelist practices the same arts under cover of the same ideals. And of course the avowed subjectivity of the encyclopedist Diderot yields to objectivity, or more accurately, its mask.

Immediately, however, Flaubert appears. The first great proletarian revolt, in 1848, marked the turning point of the century. To a large extent, a clear conscience and fixed values are already beginning to break down. The "we" that opens *Madame Bovary* and closes it (for the last sentences of the book, in the present indicative, similarly clarify the position of the writer as very much inside the world he's describing, and no longer in some empyrean of absolute knowledge), the improbable objects outside the economy of meaning, like Charles's monstrous cap (O my lovely bowler!), the strange holes in the narrative, which we'll come back to—all this shows that the novel is again being called into question. And this time things will move fast.

And yet it's impossible to regard Balzac as a brief interlude. If he remains a supreme, conclusive example (hence the historical importance that must be accorded this monumental work, even when it's so heavy it slips out of our hands), if he has become a symbol of perfect ease in the bosom of his meretricious system, "realism," it must also be said that this system has persisted despite everything down to the present day; and indeed it is this literary trend that still finds favor with the general public and traditional criticism.

In fact, from the middle of the nineteenth century, two families of novelists will develop along parallel lines: on the one hand, those who will persist—since bourgeois values are still in place, in Rome as in Moscow, even if no one believes in them anymore—in constructing narratives codified once and for all according to a sub-Balzacian realist ideology, with no contradictions or gaps in the meaningful plot; and on the other hand, those who will explore, going further with each decade, insoluble tensions, ruptures, narrative aporias, fractures, voids, etc., because they know that reality begins at the precise moment when meaning becomes uncertain.

And so, moved by the comforting familiarity of the world, I may very well act as if everything bore the face of Man and Reason (with capital letters). And in that case I'll write like the Sagans of the world, make films like the Truffauts. Why not? Or else, quite the reverse, shocked by the astonishing strangeness of the world, I'll experiment to the point of anguish with the absence from the depths of which I myself speak, and soon I'll recognize that the very details making up the reality of the world in which I live are nothing but gaps in the continuity of its received meanings, all other details being by definition ideological. At last I am able to shift uneasily between the two poles.

Someone (I forget who) has said that *Madame Bovary*, in a complete break with the preceding half-century, where everything rests on plenitude and solidity, is the precursor of the New Novel, "a crossroads of gaps and misunderstandings." And Flaubert himself writes of Emma after the famous ball that should have fulfilled her, "Her journey to Vaubyessard had made a hole in her life, like one of those great crevasses that a storm will sometimes carve in the mountains in a single night." This theme of the void, the fault, is all the more remarkable here since it immediately reappears twice more as soon as we turn the page.

Emma is daydreaming over the Vicomte's cigar case, found on the way home. She imagines the breath of the embroiderer passing through the stitching in the canvas stretched on its frame, the threads of colored silk going from hole to hole, their constantly interrupted paths interweaving to form the pattern. Isn't this an exact metaphor for the work of the modern novelist (*Flaubert, c'est moi!*) on the tattered woof of reality, the writing and then the reading moving from gap to gap to construct the narrative?

I'm even more convinced of this twenty lines later, when Emma, who has just bought a street map of Paris so she can walk around the capital without leaving her room in the provinces, traces with her fingertip multiple complex walks, stopping at the intersecting lines of the streets "in front of the blank squares that represent houses." The author's insistent repetition of the image of an imaginary journey between "blanks," gaps, helps us see the extent to which the identification he proclaimed with his heroine was in fact much more than a vague, insignificant whim.

It is thanks to the shifting holes in the texture of his novel that the text lives, like a territory in the game of Go, which only stays alive if you're careful to leave at least one empty space, a vacant square, what the experts call an open eye, or a liberty. If, on the contrary, all the places marked out by intersecting lines have pieces on them, the territory is dead, the enemy can seize it simply by encircling it.

Here we find one of Einstein's fundamental ideas, popularized a few years ago by Karl Popper: the scientific criterion for testing a theory, in whatever field, is not that it can be verified as correct by each new experiment, but quite the opposite, that in one case at least it can be proved false. Thus Marxism-Leninism and orthodox psychoanalysis, Popper says, are wrongly considered sciences by their adherents, since these disciplines are *always* right. Closed systems, they leave no space unoccupied, no area of uncertainty, no suspension of meaning, no question without answer. Science is incompatible with this totalitarian frame of mind: it can only be living, and so there must be gaps. The same goes for the literature that interests me.

And so Nikolai Stavrogin returns, the "empty center" moving ceaselessly inside *The Possessed*. He's not a devil among devils, he's the devil incarnate: the missing devil, the devil who is *lacking*. He is almost always absent from the actual scene, and we only know of his movements (offstage, abroad) through scant fragments reported second- or thirdhand by shady messengers who never reveal or understand their meaning. From time to time he erupts into the foreground of events; before astounded witnesses he then carries out some strange, unexpected act, he utters a few disjointed, inexplicable words as unintelligible to his family or to the police as to the conspirators whose chief he seems more or less to be. Everyone assumes there must be an underlying reason for his behavior, but we try in vain to discover it in the succession of riddles wantonly multiplied in his wake.

At the very end of the book we find today the condemned chapter that the Russian editor originally left out lest it give offense, and we no longer know where it goes since the rest of the chapters were renumbered consecutively by the author himself, who thus destroyed the sign that revealed the lack. Consequently, in all recent editions Stavrogin, who has already died in the preceding pages, comes back to make his confession to Bishop Tikhon. And to give it more precision, he's even written it down in a notebook . . . from which he tears a couple of pages at the last minute in front of the astonished bishop. And the reader, like Tikhon, will never know what was in those pages, although he guesses they're of the utmost importance.

The narrator, to conclude (as it were!) the erratic chapter thus mutilated, and the whole of the volume with it, makes only this comment: It's a pity that

Stavrogin tore out the two pages in question, for if he hadn't we might at last have understood the meaning of his apparently incoherent behavior, and of his whole life; on the other hand, since he always lied, from start to finish, he must have been lying in his confession too; and doubtless he was also lying in the pages he removed.

I hadn't read *The Devils* when I was writing *Le Voyeur*. And yet it's as if I wanted to reproduce the same forbidden void, the same central cavity, the same silence at the heart of my own novel, but this time using the void as the generative force of the whole text—which is not the case with Dostoyevsky. On this subject, I repeat once more that the "blank page" in *Le Voyeur* (between the first and second parts of the narrative), which seems to be there as the tangible sign of a lack, with an insistence I find crude, is in fact the result of simple typographical considerations: if the first part had been a few lines longer, the page in question would have been filled— more or less—like the others.

We didn't go to the cinema very often when I was a child, and so I was all the more impressed by the rare films I did see. One of them even gave me such nightmares the whole of the following month and long after that we had to resort to the linctus of bromide again. It was *The Invisible Man* with Franchot Tone, in the mid-thirties. And I still remember a few images where the unseen presence of a mad murderer was enough to agonize a little boy already far too susceptible to crimes committed by a sort of void in the continuity of the world. For example, the driver who thinks he's alone behind the wheel on a deserted road, having at last escaped the death that's pursuing him, is strangled with his own scarf by the invisible passenger who's been hidden in the back since he left. In the end, trapped in a hut surrounded by virgin snow, the criminal tries to flee: all we see are his footsteps slowly advancing; the gunfire of detectives hidden in the bushes; the shape of an absent body outlined in the snow.

Toward the end of that decade Corinthe too often talked about "disappearing," though we didn't quite understand whether he meant physical flight or perhaps a vague metaphysical annihilation—entering some religious order, for example (Christian, Buddhist, or God knows what). At least he wasn't the kind of man to commit suicide. "I am going," he would say, "I'm getting the hell out ...," and sometimes he would add, "through the interior," which I think was part of a quotation from a book he'd read in his youth. Like many hot-headed intellectuals of the time, he was strongly impressed by the ceremonies of the National Socialist cult in Nuremberg. He made vehement, irrational speeches about the mission of the Third Reich, which was battling the red beast prophesied by Saint John in the Apocalypse, and in a sort of delirium he confused Hitler's mass rallies with a production of *Parsifal* he'd seen in Bayreuth.

A reliable witness who met him in Bavaria at the time describes him as a sort of living corpse, half dead, a ghost. Cadaverous, or more accurately bodiless, he sits at his desk cluttered with old papers that must be the constantly reworked drafts of the manuscript, now lost (the most prestigious Parisian publishers might have had something to do with that), that he's been working on for ages. Although it's summer, he's huddled in a sort of shawl pulled up around his neck; from this meager heap emerges a face all bone, immobile, like a mummy suddenly relieved of its wrappings, as in the opening of the film I just mentioned; he has dark rings under glazed eyes wide with fever, his thin lips hardly move when he speaks. He calls to mind the famous Impressionist painting of Edouard Manneret at his work table. Without the slightest gesture despite the vehemence of his words, he talks to his visitor that day fanatically, crazily, about the rising tide, the trailing seaweed, the gaps between the rocks where the treacherous water swirls, spindrift streaking the surface . . .

I also see on rereading my notes that his son must have been a fellow student of mine at the Institut National Agronomique. I don't know at what stage of my work I could have scrawled those few hurried sentences, which don't seem to belong anywhere. It's been so long since I began to write this document about an increasingly elusive subject that I often find it impossible to identify the countless secret allusions scattered throughout the old sections, which were written almost ten years ago. In any case, I don't remember anything about the supposed presence of a young Corinthe beside me in the lecture halls, facing the gaudy frescoes of Oudot and Brianchon. I'd have to check the class lists in the college yearbook.

Nothing. I find nothing. I tirelessly reknot the broken threads of a tapestry that unravels itself at the same time, so that the pattern can hardly be discerned. Soon it will all be effaced. As for the purpose, I've always known that "the real writer has nothing to say." Moreover, my very first article on literature, published in *Critique* even before *Les Gommes* came out, began with that same sentence. It dealt with a short novel by an unknown writer about the futile obsession with the blank page; the author (I've forgotten his name), who was then Sartre's private secretary, went on to become the journalist for *L'Express* whose dishonest intervention concerning my plane crash has already been mentioned. But the opening words of my little note on his book were considered scandalous by the editors of *Critique* and omitted on publication. Jean Piel has always maintained that Georges Bataille was responsible for this curious piece of censorship, which surprises me since he didn't have much to do with the editing of the review in the fifties.

Besides, this is Flaubert's idea once more. And here again the break takes place in midcentury. It's been said that Balzac is the last happy writer, the one whose work coincides with the values of the society that nourishes him, and this is because he is the last innocent writer: he does indeed have something to say, and he eagerly amasses dozens of novels, thousands of pages, without appearing to ask himself the least question as to the validity of this strange, paradoxical exercise: writing the world. Flaubert, in three books that took him a lifetime to write, discovers both the terrifying freedom of the writer, the vanity of claiming to express original ideas, and finally the impossibility of writing, which comes only from silence and goes only toward its own particular silence.

Thus the novel's content (saying something new, Balzac thought) can actually only consist in the banality of the always-already-said: a string of stereotypes lacking originality by definition. The only meanings are those established in advance by society. But these "received ideas" (which we now call ideology) will nevertheless be the only possible material for the construction of a work of art—novel, poem, essay—empty architecture entirely held up by its form. The substance and originality of the text will come solely from the organization of its elements, which are of no interest in themselves. The writer's freedom (that is, man's freedom) resides only in the infinite complexity of possible combinations. Hasn't nature constructed all living systems, from the amoeba to the human brain, out of only eight amino acids and four nucleotides, always the same?

In *Obliques* or elsewhere I've already talked about the genesis of the film *L'Eden et après*, created out of twelve themes from the centuries-old modern panoply (the labyrinth, the dance, the double, water, the door, etc.), each repeated ten times but in a different order to form ten consecutive sequences, a bit like Schoenberg's serial music. While we were shooting and editing the film, the physical work (plus the creativity triggered by an infectious euphoria) constantly fed—and upset—this generative schema, whose rigidity is no longer apparent in the finished product, even to me. Initially there was no script, only an anecdote written in dialogue form for a first sequence in twelve frames; the one hundred and eight remaining frames were produced in collaboration with the film crew, in particular thanks to the enthusiastic contributions of the chief cameraman, Igor Luther, and the actress Catherine Jourdan, who soon became, on her own initiative, the star of the film.

Obviously chance immediately came into play, producing, for instance, after a cluster of fortuitous incidents, the improbable, miraculous appearance of the heroine's "double," an almost identical twin who even wore the same clothes. As for the theme of "blood," which had just played an important part in the first three weeks of filming in the Slovak state studios, it suddenly took on an unexpected dimension in real life.

We're in Bratislava at the end of August 1969. For the last six days we've been struggling to perfect the set of the Eden café: a labyrinthine system of panels inspired by Mondrian that slide across the whole set on a grid of parallel rails and can be moved after each take or sometimes even during shooting in order to make the space even more fluid. On Saturday evening I have a chance to drink an after-dinner carafe of white wine in a strip-tease bar (a legacy of the Prague Spring, as was my contract) where I can choose a nude extra for the following Tuesday. Catherine and my Tunisian assistant are both tired and leave early. I stay on with Catherine Jourdan (I just call her Jourdan to avoid confusion), a young French actor, and an official of the Tunisian co-production company.

As we're walking back to our hotel through the deserted city about midnight, happy and relaxed, we make a few obviously silly jokes about a small Soviet plane on display opposite the Carlton in a gesture of provocation. When we reach the main entrance to this luxuriously antiquated building (we're staying at the more modern Dévin, three hundred meters away on the Danube), a police patrol accosts us; perhaps they noticed our irreverent behavior, although it was harmless enough.

Considering myself responsible for the little group, I cheerfully undertake to justify our late-night stroll. Besides, there isn't a curfew. The Franco-Czech film I'm making is under the official auspices of the nationalized film industry. And a few days before I'd even been given the local decoration that corresponds to our Arts-et-Lettres. But as I only know a few words of the language, I make the mistake of muddling through in German, and they doubtless take us for Austrian tourists (Vienna is a few kilometers away on the opposite bank of the river) who've come to live it up on the cheap thanks to our abominable capitalist hard cash. To make matters worse, my hair is much too long for a good average Communist, and I'd forgotten to shave that morning (I didn't have a beard at the time, only a moustache, also Western).

Two of the policemen are in uniform, three others in plain clothes. All five have crew cuts and shaven necks, but they're very red in the face, probably drunk. It is the exact anniversary of the entry of the Warsaw Pact troops, who had come precisely to put an end to the general license; the authorities are afraid that commemorative demonstrations may be held, and rumor has it that they've been priming their most loyal troops, the more excitable of whom are obviously spoiling for a fight. One of the plainclothesmen asks for my papers; I hand them over.

But at the same moment his neighbor, who has American-style brass knuckles on his right hand, brandishes a canister with his left and squirts a few jets of tear gas into my face. He immediately starts punching me in the jaw. Completely dazed, I lean back against the wall of the Carlton while—I was told later—tracing vague flourishes in the air, as if I were drowsily chasing insects away in slow motion, which of course does nothing to ward off the well-aimed blows that continue to rain down on my face. My two male companions stand stock-still watching the massacre, intimidated by the soldiers. It is Jourdan who intervenes: she thrusts her delicate face in front of mine to protect me, staring defiantly at my attacker. For a moment the man hesitates to disfigure this pretty girl. His armed fist falls to his side.

My identity card is returned to me in silence, as if after some banal routine check. And we're left to go on our way undisturbed. It all happened as if in a dream, with no explanation, no shouting, no confusion; I'm tempted to say with no violence, since the world seems wrapped in cotton wool, including the metal weapon whose repeated blows to my jaw I hardly felt, doubtless anesthetized by the gas. But when I get to my room I realize by Catherine's expression that I must be seriously injured.

I look at myself in the bathroom mirror: I have two broken teeth in the upper jaw on the left, another that's loose, and deep cuts above and below the mouth; my white shirt is three-quarters red from collar to waist (lip wounds bleed a lot), the shape of the bloodstains ironically recalling a cruel scene filmed in the studio that morning. As I gradually recover with the help of towels soaked in cold water, I remember the shape of the canister the policeman used: it bears a curious resemblance to a small object (meant to scare off troublemakers) already on one of the reels of my film (but that sequence was finally shown only in an anagrammatic version for television that had a random rather than a sequential structure and was called *N. a pris les dés*).

From dawn onward the whole production team is in an uproar. I make the acquaintance of the free health-care system of the so-called true Socialist countries: a party functionary goes everywhere with me to slip hundred-crown notes to the nurses who admit me and the surgeons who examine me or sew me up. And then the authorities are quick to reassure me: I mustn't be upset by a mere misunderstanding, the valiant guardians of law and order just didn't know who I was! This confirms me in my first impression: as usual this whole affair that happened to me really had nothing to do with me . . .

Another image, which must come from the following days: the dentist leaning over me—who in a bitter profession of anti-Communist faith strongly advises me to have the necessary denture made in France—yells in my face his diagnosis concerning the incisor that at first seemed to be the least damaged as he vigorously manhandles the root: "Ah! Ah! It's loose, Monsieur Engineer! *Elle bouge!*" he repeats in French, grimacing and laughing uproariously.

I remember that close woman friend with whom my mother must have been in love (or vice versa), a dental surgeon in Brest. She always took care of our teeth when we were children, and her gentleness and skill added to the charm of her (to us) very luxurious apartment, where she played "The Sunken Cathedral" on an ebony grand piano. It was she who told me about the strange wound that Henri de Corinthe had on his neck: two little red holes about a centimeter apart that she found when she was taking out a wisdom tooth.

Corinthe died in Finistère a short while later. My father went to his funeral, a civil funeral with an illicit mass celebrated by an unfrocked priest, held in the open air outside the closed church door. It took place in a little town on the west coast, something like Porsmoguer-en-Plouarzel, where Comte Henri lived alone at the bottom of an old gun emplacement from the time of Vauban, built into the cliff (you had to go down a stone staircase to get to the rooms); he had bought it from the state and furnished it in a very Spartan fashion. So he had been excommunicated. For how long? Why? The small procession stopped in a sort of parish close opposite the silent bell tower. A fine cold drizzle had been falling since the day before. It was the end of autumn. The men knelt down in their dark suits on the sodden earth. When my father described it on his return to Les Roches Noires, I thought of "the fog and damp of the humanist conscience."

It was almost dark already. We'd just had our tea, which was a daily ritual. When my father stopped speaking, Grandmother, who was over ninety and forgot everything instantly, asked, "Well, aren't we having tea today?" Her daughter answered her irritably: "We've just had it. Tea's over!" After a moment's thought, with the haughty air now inseparable from her bewilderment, Grandmother said as if to herself, "Nonsense, you idiot! Tea's never over."